A Short History of the Mass

D1628466

Catholic Truth Society

First published 1983 by the
Incorporated Catholic Truth Society
38–40 Eccleston Square
London SW1V 1PD

ISBN 085183 512 0

AC

Printed and bound in England by
Staples Printers Rochester Limited
at The Stanhope Press

Contents

Contents

Introduction

Even though the rite of the Mass has been simplified since the Second Vatican Council it still appears somewhat complicated. In writing a history of the Mass, then, it is necessary to understand its fundamental pattern or shape. The Council's Constitution on the Liturgy, *Sacrosanctum Concilium* (referred to hereafter as CL) (n. 56) indicates what this is. The Mass consists of two parts: the liturgy of the word and the liturgy of the eucharist. They are so closely connected that they constitute one single act of worship, but these two parts have histories of their own and, to some extent, each will have to be studied separately.

Again, in considering the liturgy of the eucharist we need to isolate its core, that is, its principal element. This, as the General Instruction attached to the Roman Missal of 1970 says, is the eucharistic prayer, 'the climax and the very heart of the entire celebration' (n. 54). It is with this, then, that we begin, and we pursue its history up to the third century. After this we give an account of the history of the liturgy of the word for the same period. A brief explanation of the divergence of the liturgical rites which began to take shape in different parts of the Church in the fourth century follows. After that we study the Roman rite from the fourth to the seventh century. The Carolingian reform of the eighth–ninth centuries, when the rite was adapted to non-Roman conditions north of the Alps, is then considered. A second turning point is the organisation of the rite in the early thirteenth century, which carries us on to the revision that took place after the Council of Trent (1545–1563). For four hundred years thereafter only minor changes took place, until the revision decreed by the

Second Vatican Council. This will be reviewed in the light of the foregoing history.

A number of references in the text are intended to support certain possibly contentious statements. There are references to ancient liturgical texts and these will be found in the collection PEER: *Prayers of the Eucharist. Early and Reformed* (eds. R. C. D. Jasper and G. J. Cuming).

The purpose of this book is to give a necessarily brief account of the development of the Mass. Commentary on the meaning of the Roman rite of 1970 will be found in the *General Instruction on the Roman Missal* and in books mentioned in the Reading List.

I gratefully acknowledge the help Father Henry Ashworth O.S.B. of Quarr Abbey gave to me only a short time before his unexpected and much lamented death in October 1980. I wish to thank Father Abbot, the Right Reverend Aelred Sillem, and members of his community for giving me the free run of their excellent library. Finally, I owe a debt of gratitude to W. Jardine Grisbrooke, lecturer in liturgy at Oscott College, who kindly read a first draft of the book and saved me from a number of errors. If any remain they are my own.

J.D.C.

1.

Origins

All Christians are agreed that the holy eucharist, which in the West is now usually called the Mass, had its origins in the Last Supper, when Jesus said over the bread, 'This is my body . . .' and gave it to his disciples, and when he said over the wine, 'This is the blood of the covenant . . .' and gave it to them to drink. But this simple ceremony seems a long way from the Mass as we know it, and if we are to find the origins of the *liturgy* of the Mass we must look at what is known of contemporary Jewish meal-customs.

More than thirty years ago the well known liturgical scholar Dom Gregory Dix pointed out that the liturgy of the eucharist as it emerges into the light of history has a pattern or 'shape' consisting of four actions: the taking, the blessing, the breaking, and the giving. That is, the 'president' takes the bread and wine, says the 'blessing' over them, breaks the bread and gives the bread and wine in communion. This model has been widely accepted, and provides a useful basis for an examination of the origins of the eucharist and the development of the Mass.

Although it is commonly thought that the Last Supper was a Passover meal (cf. Matthew 25:17; Mark 14:14; Luke 22:7–15; but see also John 18:28) it is not necessarily this meal that provided the pattern for the rite of the eucharist. For one thing the Passover meal, at least as it is known in rather later documents, was somewhat complicated, and for another it was an annual celebration and could hardly have been the model for the eucharist, which we know from the New Testament was celebrated frequently, almost certainly every week. Furthermore, within New Testament times the Christian Sunday had replaced the Jewish Sabbath (which began on Friday evening), and it is most probable

1

that the eve-of-Sabbath meal provided the framework of the eucharistic rite.

At this meal there were two table-prayers, one at the beginning and one at the end, rather like grace before and after our meals. Some indication that this was how the primitive eucharist was celebrated can be gathered from the accounts of Paul and Luke, where we read that the words over the bread came at the beginning of the meal and those over the wine 'after supper' (I Corinthians 11:23–36; Luke 22:19–20). St Paul, writing about 55 AD, shows that the meal still existed. Some time later the meal had been displaced and the two consecrations had been combined, as we see from Matthew 26:26–28 and Mark 14:22–24.

We can gain further information from the table prayers. There is first however a small matter of terminology we need to consider. The term 'blessing' in Hebrew usage did not mean the blessing *of* a person or object but the 'blessing of God' for his gifts. Its sense survives in the Latin *'bene-dicere'* which means to 'say-well' of someone, in this case God. And the form it took was to proclaim the names of God, and is equivalent to our word 'praise'. We and the Jews 'bless God' or 'praise him' for his gifts or for something he has done for us. For 'thanks' there was a quite different Hebrew word, as of course with us.

The first table-prayer, then, was a 'blessing' of God because he had provided the food of the earth, and after the leader (the father of the family) had said the words he broke pieces off the loaf he was holding and handed them to those who were present. This was said and done at the beginning of the meal.

The second, longer and more important prayer that came at the end of the meal began, 'Let us give thanks to the Lord (our God),' these last two words being added when there were a hundred or more people present. The prayer, taking up the word 'thanks', continued: 'We thank you, Lord our God, for giving us a good and pleasant land ... for the covenant, for the Law, life and food. ...' On certain great feasts (of which the Passover was the greatest) an insertion, or *embolism,* was made recalling the saving deeds of God in the past, and the prayer ended with supplication to God to have mercy on his people and save them. After this there was a short *doxology,* blessing (i.e. praising) God.[1]

---

[1] Thomas J. Talley, 'From Berakah to Eucharistia' in *Worship,* Vol. 50, no. 2, March, 1976, pp. 115–137.

It is not difficult to discern in these prayers the outline of the eucharistic prayer. There is the invitation, 'Let us give thanks ...' as in our liturgy, there is the 'taking' of the bread and the giving of praise, there is the thanksgiving for the saving deeds of God in Christ, there is the recalling of the past deeds of salvation, and there is supplication that leaves the way open for the petitions that (usually) come at the end of the prayer and perhaps (less certainly) for the invocation of the Holy Spirit, later called the *epiclesis*.

It was to these two table-prayers that Jesus attached the words, 'This is my body ...' and, 'This is my blood of the covenant ...' respectively, the latter phrase recalling, it seems, the convenant mentioned in the second table-prayer. As the Roman Canon makes clear, this was the 'new and eternal covenant' which Jesus was inaugurating. Even when the two prayers were combined to make one, as in Matthew and Mark, the memory of them was retained for there we read that Jesus 'blessed' the bread (i.e. said the prayer of blessing over it) and 'gave thanks' over the wine (i.e. said the prayer of thanksgiving over it). Nor did this memory entirely fade. As we read in an old eucharistic prayer of St Basil, Jesus is said to 'bless' the bread and to 'give thanks' over the wine. But the term 'thanks' rapidly came to dominate the institution narrative. In the accounts of Paul and Luke, as well as in other texts of the second century, the word 'blessed' has disappeared, though in the great eucharistic prayers it is transformed into the praise of God, particularly notable in the eucharistic prayers of St James and St Basil and in the 'prefaces' of the Roman rite. The word 'to give thanks' (*eucharistein*) remained to become the name of the whole service. That this was so can be gathered from the earliest description we have of the eucharist outside the New Testament: the 'president' praises and glorifies God, the Father of all things, in the name of the Son and the Holy Spirit and then makes a long prayer of thanksgiving.

Accompanying the words were two actions: the wine was mixed with water, and the leader raised the cup a hand's breadth above the table. These two actions are still found in the Roman rite, and the mixing of the chalice is common to almost all rites.

The eucharist in the second century

The first description of the eucharist is given by St Justin the Martyr, who wrote in Rome about the year 150. Of the eucharistic

3

prayer he records that the 'president' (*proestōs*) of the assembly said extemporaneously a prayer of some length over the bread and wine, and at the end of it all the people replied, 'Amen'. It is clear that the prayer continued without interruption until the people received communion at the end of it. There is no reason to suppose that Justin was saying anything new. He was a convert, he had made his way from Palestine to Rome, he was familiar with the customs of the Church in the East and in the West, and so his evidence takes us back to the years before 150.

Since Justin gives only a general description of the eucharist we cannot be sure of all the details. But in what seems to be a commentary on his own description, referring to the bread and the wine mixed with water, he says, 'this food is called by us "eucharist"' and then he gives the words of institution. What is done, he says, comes down from the apostles who were obeying Christ when he said, 'This is my body' and, 'This is my blood'. Here and elsewhere he insists that in the eucharist the Church is making the memorial (*anamnesis*) of what Christ did at the Last Supper and in his passion. He also reveals that 'praise and glory' are offered to the Father of all things, through the name of his Son and of the Holy Spirit.[2]

Do we know anything more about the eucharist in these early days? In a document called the *Didache* (*The Teaching of the Twelve Apostles*) there is reference in two places (9 and 14) to what seems to be the eucharist. In the first passage a thanksgiving meal is described, but scholars are more and more coming to the view that there are elements here of the eucharist strictly so called. It begins, 'About the eucharist, give thanks in this way ...' and the prayers that follow, though Jewish in form, are Christian in language and content. God is thanked (not 'blessed') for the gifts of wine and bread (in that order) and there is a prayer for the unity of the Church. A thanksgiving after the meal ends with *Hosanna*, an invitation to those who are worthy to come forward (and to repentance to those who are not), and finally *Maranatha*, 'Come, Lord' (cf. I Corinthians 16:22; Apocalypse 22:20). If there was no eucharistic prayer that is perhaps because it was extemporised. The 'charismatics' were allowed 'to give thanks' freely.

[2] For texts see PEER, pp. 18–20. *Apology* I, 65, 66, 67; *Dialogue with Trypho*, 117,1.

In the second passage (14) there are distinctly liturgical features:

(i) The celebration takes place on the Lord's day (Sunday).
(ii) The people 'come together', i.e. they make the *synaxis* (the assembly).
(iii) They confess their sins so that their 'sacrifice may be pure'.
(iv) They break bread and give thanks.
(v) There is the kiss of peace.
(vi) The service is called 'sacrifice' three times in a very short passage which ends with a quotation from Malachi 1:11, always understood in the early Church as referring to the eucharistic sacrifice.

In this account there is the *presence* of a meal and the (apparent) *absence* of readings from the scriptures. When we turn to Justin we find that the meal has dropped away and the readings of the scriptures are part of the service. He gives two accounts of the eucharist, to the first of which was attached the celebration of baptism; the second is of the ordinary Sunday service.

From these we can deduce the following:

(i) The people meet on Sunday.
(ii) There are readings from the 'memoirs' of the apostles or the writings of the prophets 'for as long as time allows'.
(iii) The president preaches a homily.
(iv) All stand and 'prayers' are offered (i.e. the general intercessions).
(v) The kiss of peace is exchanged.
(vi) The bread, and the wine mixed with water, are brought to the president, who takes them.
(vii) The president says the prayer of thanksgiving over them and all the people give their assent saying, 'Amen'.
(viii) Everyone receives communion and deacons take it to those who are absent.
(ix) There is a collection to provide for orphans and widows and any in need.

Here, at this early date, clearly recognizable, are the main lines of the Mass. There is the liturgy or ministry of the word, viz. readings from both Old and New Testaments, the homily, and the intercessions which, as we known from 1 Timothy 2:2, included 'petitions and intercessions' for kings and others in authority. The liturgy of the eucharist is simple and straightforward: the bread and wine are brought forward (and no doubt placed on the table), the president recites the eucharistic prayer 'as well as he is able' (it was not written down), the people reply 'Amen' and immediately receive communion. There is no mention of the Lord's Prayer, but communion is taken to the 'absent' (those who are ill?) by the proper minister, i.e. the deacon. As for the collection, the Church for centuries had on its 'pay-roll' large numbers of people in need and this is why the collection was taken.

Three further remarks are called for.

First, it is to be noted that the kiss of peace is exchanged before the eucharist proper begins. This is its original place and was no doubt suggested by Matthew 5:23–24, where we are told to be reconciled with our neighbour before making our offering at the altar.

Secondly, it has often been said that the ministry of the word was only added to the eucharist sometime before Justin wrote. This is improbable. At the Last Supper there were the many words of Jesus, among them the recalling in the second part of the 'thanksgiving' (inserted at Passover time) of the first Passover, the deliverance from Egypt, the passage through the Red Sea and, above all, the (old) covenant. Then when the Risen Christ met the two disciples on the way to Emmaus he first expounded the scriptures and then broke bread (Luke 24:27–30), and St Paul in his recommendations about the use of the charismatic gifts says that 'everyone is to be ready with a psalm or a sermon or a revelation' at all their meetings (I Corinthians 14:26). Again, when he celebrated the 'breaking of the bread' at Troas (Acts 20:7–11) he preached a long sermon 'until midnight'. And it is commonly thought that his letters, which so often end with a liturgical formula (cf. 2 Corinthians 13:12–13; Thessalonians 5:27–28; Colossians 3:15–16; Romans 16:16, etc.), were read out at the eucharistic assemblies. We can be sure then that passages from the Old Testament (which was the 'Bible' at this time) and the Letters of St Paul and the other apostles were read at the early eucharistic celebrations. What seems to have happened, perhaps after the destruction of the Temple in AD 70, is that the Church adopted the synagogue service, which consisted of readings from the Law (the first five books of the Old Testament), the prophets and other writings, and the recitations of psalms and certain prayers. To these, before Justin's time, had been added the 'memoirs' of the apostles, no doubt the gospels, which began to circulate in collections in the early part of the second century.

Even so, the ministry of the word has an identity of its own. The Constitution on the Liturgy (n. 7) is doing no more than echo the tradition when it says that Christ is present when the gospel is proclaimed in church (CL 7,33). Later on in Rome, on days when the eucharist was not celebrated, namely on some Wednesdays and Fridays, there was always a ministry of the word. It is likely, then, that from earliest times the eucharist was normally accompanied by a ministry of the word. Possible exceptions to the rule were the occasions when baptisms (Justin) and ordinations (Hippolytus) were administered in the eucharistic liturgy.

Thirdly, and finally, it is noteworthy that Justin does not mention 'the breaking of the bread'. This does not mean that it did not exist (his description of the rite is not complete), but we must say a word about it now. The breaking of the bread, which had become a technical term for the eucharist in the New Testament, was a practical necessity. The loaf had to be broken up so that all might communicate from it. But it had also a deep symbolic significance which is given by St Paul: 'Although we are many we are all one body because we have received from the one loaf (*artos*)' (I Corinthians 10:17).[3]

The oldest eucharistic prayer

As we have seen, Justin speaks of the eucharistic prayer but does not give a text, as none as yet existed. It was improvised, as indeed it continued to be in the West until towards the end of the fourth century. The oldest known *text*, at least in the West,[4] is to be found in the writings of a priest called Hippolytus, who lived in Rome and is thought to have composed the prayer about AD 215. He wrote in Greek but the prayer survives in a Latin translation, as well as in other versions, more or less accurate, Coptic, Ethiopian, Arabic and Syriac. These versions witness to the popularity of the prayer and show that there was a certain unity, at least of structure, in the liturgy of the first three centuries. This is also

[3] In the contex 'loaf' seems to be the right translation of the Greek 'artos', cf. RSV, *in loco.*

[4] There is the prayer of Addai and Mari which is probably of the middle of the third century. It is without the institution-narrative though some scholars think that it originally had one.

attested by the invitiation made about 154 by Pope Anicetus to Polycarp, bishop of Smyrna in Asia Minor, to celebrate the eucharist when on a visit to Rome.

The prayer of Hippolytus is now familiar to us as it appears, with one or two important changes, as eucharistic prayer II, in the Roman Missal of 1970. A brief consideration will allow us to see what the old Latin version was and what changes have been made. It begins with the dialogue as we still have it, except that it has 'Let us give thanks to the Lord', which is the shorter of the two forms given in the texts of the Jewish table-prayers. The most notable difference is that it has no *Sanctus*. It runs right on from beginning to end without interruption. It is unusual, too, in having no reference to salvation history in the Old Testament and concentrates on the saving deeds of Christ in the New Testament. The institution narrative is short, though the words over the bread include the Lukan 'broken for you'. There follows the 'making of the memory', i.e. the *anamnesis* of the death and resurrection, and the offering of 'the bread and the cup'. In the Latin text of the Verona MS (probably of the sixth century) there is an *epiclesis,* i.e. an invocation of the Holy Spirit, on the 'offering' (*oblationem*) and on the communicants that, filled with the Holy Spirit, they may be made one and strengthened in faith.

Whether or not the prayer of Hippolytus owes anything to the Jewish prayers it is profoundly Christian. We note its Trinitarian pattern: thanks are given to the Father 'through your Child (servant) Jesus', and at the end praise and glory are given to the Father 'through the Son with the Holy Spirit'. It is a pattern that will be found in almost all future eucharistic prayers.

Hippolytus sets his prayer in the context of the ordination of a bishop, priest (presbyter) and deacon, and does not give any indication of the existence of a ministry of the word. In a futher description of the rites of Christian initiation he shows that there were readings, that the Prayer of the Faithful existed and that the kiss of peace was given before the eucharistic action began. The newly baptised made their offering, took part in the Mass for the first time and received communion after the eucharistic prayer.

Although Hippolytus gives his prayer only as a model, and although anything like a fixed liturgy was a long way off, we may take it that he gives us a true, if incomplete, picture of the liturgy in Rome in the first two decades of third century.

The other notable differences between the prayer of Hippolytus and the prayer we say at Mass today are:

(a) the division of eucharistic prayer II into two parts by the *Sanctus*;

(b) the connecting passage with an invocation of the Holy Spirit on the offerings;

(c) the harmonisation of the institution-narrative and the doxology with those in the other three eucharistic prayers;

(d) the addition of the intercessions.[5]

---

[5] For a translation of the prayer of Hippolytus see PEER, pp. 21–25.

2.

The Development of Different Rites

As will be remembered, during the first two hundred and fifty years of its existence the Church was an 'illegal religion' in the Roman Empire, and from time to time suffered persecution. This, however, did not stop the growth of the Church and by the end of the third century Christians were numerous throughout the Empire. Local communities for the most part remained small, but there were fully organised Churches, for instance in Rome and North Africa. With the possible exceptions of Spain and North Africa Greek was still the common language, and communication was maintained between the East and West. There was also some liturgical development: the catechumenate, by which candidates for Christian initiation were prepared, was fully organised in the third century. Even so, in the liturgy of the eucharist a certain unity was preserved, though it was a unity of pattern rather than a uniformity of detail. As we have seen, the eucharistic prayer of Hippolytus, with a few additions, circulated in the East. By the end of the fourth century however there was a considerable diversity of rites and we are prompted to ask how this came about.

The causes of diversity

Not all is clear in this matter but there seem to have been three factors, political, cultural and theological, making for diversification.

The political factor

With the victory of the Emperor Constantine in 312 over the forces of paganism the Church moved into a new era. From being a persecuted minority it became gradually the Church of the Empire. Greater organisation became possible and necessary. How was the Church that stretched from Syria in the East to Spain and Britain in the West to be governed? The answer is to be seen in the emergence of the three great patriarchates of Antioch, Alexandria and Rome. These bishoprics were important civil centres and it is understandable that they became ecclesiastical centres, a fact that was observable even before the coming of Constantine. In other words, the framework was already there, and these patriarchates were capable of conducting their own affairs. And this in fact they did, with recourse to Rome on the part of Antioch and Alexandria only in matters of the greatest importance, when the unity of faith threatened. In the fifth century Byzantium (i.e. Constantinople) founded by the Emperor, and Jerusalem, the city of the Holy Places, became patriarchates also. It was in these five centres that the families of the liturgy began to take shape.

Cultural factors

These patriarchates were also *cultural* centres, Greek-speaking for the most part, though Syriac was used in the Antioch region (including Jerusalem) and Coptic was the language of the people of Egypt, especially outside Alexandria. It was natural that they should develop liturgies that expressed their own culture.

Syriac is a language very close to Hebrew, the language of the Old Testament, and influence coming from that quarter can be detected in liturgies shaped in that region.

Although Alexandria was one of the greatest centres of Greek culture and literature of ancient times, the language of the people became Coptic, the old Egyptian language of the Pharaohs put into Greek letters (with some special symbols). Egypt was also the country where primitive monasticism originated, and the monks for the most part were Coptic-speaking. Again, Egypt had suffered particularly savage persecution under the Emperor Diocletian at the beginning of the fourth century, and it is understandable that Coptic Christians should look back to their glorious past. In other words, they tended to be conservative, and the Coptic liturgy still gives the impression of being very old.

Alexandria, on the other hand, was very open to liturgical influences, and a fourth century eucharistic prayer used there is attributed to St Basil of Cappadocia in Asia Minor. Here, and at

11

Antioch and Constantinople, there was current a certain popular Platonic philosophy that marked their eucharistic prayers. Quite naturally, they used a number of terms like 'ineffable', 'inconceivable', and 'incomprehensible' in describing God, and these remain in their prayers to this day, as can be seen from the anaphora of St John Chrysostom.[1]

The Roman patriarchate, whose sphere of influence was the whole of the West where, outside Rome and Southern Italy, Latin was the prevalent language and where philosophical considerations did not come into play, gradually developed its own style of liturgy about which we shall have much to say below.

Theological factors

Finally, there were theological factors involved in the diversification of rites. It is normal that different cultural regions of the Church should develop different insights into the one faith. This happened in the East and West. Though sharp distinctions are not wholly satisfactory, the East could be said to emphasise the transcendence of God (hence the epithets given above) and the West his immanence, 'God-with-us'. It is also true that eastern Christians had a greater awareness of the presence and action of the Holy Spirit, and this, as we shall see, is also reflected in their liturgies.

Heresies, too, played some part in liturgical formation and in the spread of certain liturgies. Arianism, which denied that Christ was truly the Son of God, equal to the Father, dominated the fourth century and had its effects even later in the West. It made people very sensitive about how they should address Jesus in the liturgy. One small example will show this. The original form of 'Glory be to the Father and to the Son and to the Holy Spirit' seems to have been, 'Glory be to the Father through the Son in the Holy Spirit.' Since this could be interpreted as putting Christ in a subordinate position to the Father it dropped out of use. To put the matter more technically, the mediatorship of Christ was somewhat obscured and prayers were frequently addressed *to* him, though this practice can be found from an early date. The heresies of Nestorius (Jesus was a God-inspired man) and of Eutyches (his humanity was swallowed up in his divinity), which were condemned at the Councils of Ephesus (431) and Chalcedon (451), led to schism and a wider diffusion of liturgies. The

[1] Cf. PEER, Liturgy of St John Chrysostom, p. 79 ff.

Nestorian Church established itself in East Syria and then in Persia and penetrated as far as South India. Fortunately, however, their liturgies were not greatly affected by their heresies.

A variety of rites

It was in this way, then, that families of liturgies grew and it should be emphasised that they are all authentic, and many of them are still in use. It will be useful to give one or two features of these liturgies since they have had their influence on the recent reform of the Roman rite.

The liturgy of Egypt, St Mark's for example, has an invocation of the Holy Spirit *before* the institution narrative. This is now to be found in all the new eucharistic prayers (II, III, IV) of the Roman Missal of 1970. In the eastern prayers, from the fourth century onwards, for instance those of St John Chrysostom, St Basil and St James (Jerusalem), there is always an invocation of the Holy Spirit *after* the words of institution and this, too, is now in our new eucharistic prayers, through there it is an invocation of the Holy Spirit on the communicants rather than on the bread and wine as in the eastern prayers. The Egyptian type of prayer was more broken up and has some affinity with the Roman Canon (eucharistic prayer I). On the other hand, the Antiochene type of prayer runs uninterruptedly from the beginning to the end rather like our eucharistic prayer IV. The *Sanctus* appears in the prayer of Sarapion of Thmuis (about 350) and is generally thought to have been inserted into other prayers subsequently to their original composition.

A word or two must also be spared for certain western rites to which we shall have to refer from time to time in what follows.

The Ambrosian rite

This rite, used, with some modifications, today in Milan, has its origins in the fourth century. It is basically Roman, having the Roman Canon (with a few differences) and retaining a number of old Roman features. Early on it would seem it acquired certain elements from Eastern and Gallican rites, notably the course of readings. St Ambrose himself said that he wished to follow the model of Rome but reserved the right to keep the customs (e.g. the washing of the feet at baptism) and ceremonies of his own Church.

The Visigothic or Mozarabic rite

Spain was rather cut off from the rest of Europe and this isolation became almost complete after the Arabic invasions of the beginning of the eighth century. Its liturgy developed on its own lines and is very ancient, some of its texts apparently going back to the fifth century. Notable features are its lack of a fixed canon, which was made up of movable prayers grouped round the institution narrative. Sometimes the *anamnesis* was wanting. The rite was very open to eastern influences. Greek phrases are found in it, the creed was first used in the West in Spain, and in some of the eucharistic prayers there is an *epiclesis* of the Holy Spirit. The Visigoths were Arians, who, as we have said, denied the divinity of Christ. Orthodox Spanish Christians vehemently resisted this heresy, and they expressed their orthodoxy in their prayers, which were addressed to Christ or to the Holy Trinity: the prayer of the former offertory rite, 'Accept Holy Trinity . . .' was from Spanish sources, as with great probability is the 'preface' of the Holy Trinity.

Today, the rite is only celebrated regularly in the Mozarabic chapel of the Cathedral of Toledo.

The Gallican rite(s)

Whether or not there was a single rite in the area that now roughly corresponds to France is not certain. Its already Romanised form of the seventh century rapidly withered away with the liturgical reform of Charlemagne at the end of the eighth century. But it had a strong resemblance to the Visigothic rite (no fixed canon), it reacted in like manner to the Arian threat and its prayers, like the Spanish, are exuberant and often addressed to the Holy Trinity or to Christ. But it retained something of its own spirit even after the Carolingian reform. It was colourful and more dramatic than the Roman rite which, in its original state, was always sober, even austere.

The Celtic rite

This has been described as a mixture of Roman, Gallican, Spanish and eastern elements and certain native compositions. The best known text is the Stowe Missal.

3.

The Emergence of the Roman Rite

Life and liturgy constantly interact on each other, and we cannot understand the form a particular rite took unless we see its development in its historical context.

When the Church gained her freedom under the Emperor Constantine in 313 she moved into the full light of day. Now great numbers of people began to come into the Church, liturgical assemblies became larger and new and bigger buildings were required. Constantine, for all his short-comings, was a generous patron and donor. Great churches like St John Lateran and St Peter's began to rise and these large and spacious basilicas demanded a more elaborate style of worship. Inevitably the Mass lost something of its former intimacy, but it was still a functional liturgy in which the whole community, the clergy in their various ranks and the people, continued to play their respective roles. This was made plain by the plan of the church. At the east end there was the apse in which was placed the bishop's chair, the *cathedra magistri*, from which he preached and taught his people. In front of him, on the chord of the apse, stood the altar completely unadorned except for a linen cloth which was put on it in the course of the service. Grouped to the left and the right of the bishop were the presbyters (much later, cardinals) of the Roman Church who celebrated with him. In front of the altar were the singers who led the congregation in singing, and filling the nave were the people who took part by response and song, by listening to the readings declaimed by the appropriate ministers and to the homily preached by the pope or presiding bishop.[1] Certainly in

[1] In some places, Jerusalem and North Africa, for example, both the priests present and the bishop preached at the same Mass!

15

North Africa, and most probably in Rome, the people presented the offerings of bread and wine for the Mass and gifts for the needy. The eucharistic action followed, about which we will have something to say later on.

From a Greek to a Latin liturgy

One of the most important changes in the liturgy of the West was the change of language. It made possible the development of a Roman rite.

The original language of the liturgy in both East and West was Greek, which was the *lingua franca* of the Roman Empire from Palestine to Southern Gaul, including of course Rome. This is clear from Justin and Hippolytus, who both wrote in Greek and worked in Rome. But by the end of the fourth century there was a fully developed liturgical Latin in which some of the prayers that still exist in our liturgy were written. When and why did the change come? For the first eight hundred years of the Church's history there was no notion that the Mass should be shrouded in mystery or that there should be only one liturgical language. Passages of the Bible were read out to be understood, the people prayed and responded in their own language, whether it was Greek, Syriac or Latin. It was taken for granted that the people should take part in the celebration of the liturgy as the priestly people of Christ. When, then, towards the end of the third century, the language generally used in Rome was changing from Greek to Latin the language of the liturgy was also changed.

It seems to have been a gradual process, for there are hints that some Greek remained in the liturgy as late as the middle of the fourth century, but by this time the eucharistic prayer was in Latin for one or two phrases are quoted from it and, as we shall see, St Ambrose gives a substantial part of that prayer a little later. Quite certainly the change of language had already been made in North Africa where, towards the end of the second century, the first translations of the Bible from Greek into Latin had been made. Moreover, St Cyprian, the Bishop of Carthage, who was martyred in 258, has phrases in his commentary on the Lord's Prayer that are almost identical to those in the invitatory to the same prayer as it stands in our liturgy to this day. He also witnesses to the existence of the *Sursum corda* ('Lift up your hearts') before the eucharistic prayer, as also does the poet

Commodian for Rome about the same time. We should also remember that St Jerome had completed his translation of the Old Testament from Hebrew into Latin by the end of the fourth century, a translation that had become necessary because there were so many discrepancies between the Latin translations already in use.[2] The Latin of St Jerome's Vulgate, as it came to be called, had a profound influence on the language of the liturgy in the West.

Against this background we will give some account of the liturgy as far as it can be discerned in the fourth century.

The liturgy of the word

The practice of reading from the scriptures, both the Old and the New Testament, was universal throughout the Church, though the number of readings varied from place to place. In fourth century Antioch, for instance, the old synagogue pattern can be discerned: there was a reading from the Law and one from the prophets followed by a reading from the epistles (or sometimes from Acts) and finally one from the gospels. In the West Syriac rite today there are six readings of which three are from the Law, the prophets and the wisdom books. In Egypt there were four readings, two from the Old Testament and two from the New, the last being from a gospel. But the most usual pattern was one reading from the Old Testament, one from the New Testament non-gospel material (epistles, Acts and Apocalypse) and one from the gospels. There is little doubt that this was also the original Roman practice, of which there are traces as late as the seventh century. But for reasons unknown to us there was a tendency both in Rome and in Constantinople to drop the Old Testament reading, notably on the greater feasts.

With the readings psalms were sung, though on the evidence available to us[3] it is difficult to say how they were related to the readings. Sometimes the psalm *preceded* the first reading; at others, for example the fast days of Lent, even when there were two or three readings, the psalm with its response followed the third. On the Vigils of Epiphany and Easter, when there were as

---

[2] He *revised* the Latin translation of the gospels but not, it seems, of the rest of the New Testament.
[3] A. G. Martimort, *Kyriakon* (Festschrift Johannes Quasten), eds. P. Garfield and J. A. Jungmann (Münster, Westfalen, 1970).

many as twelve readings, there were no psalms. The readings ended with the Canticle of Daniel which was sung because it was lyrical and was in fact a part of Morning Prayer. In the fourth century liturgy of Jerusalem, as described by Egeria,[4] the first psalm was clearly an entrance psalm and in Lent, when there were three Old Testament readings, they were followed by a psalm and there was no gospel. On some feast days there were two readings before the gospel but no psalm.

All this means that the pattern of the liturgy of the word varied a good deal, but by the end of the fourth century it seems to have become fixed. St Augustine (*Serm.* 165) says: 'We have heard the Apostle, we have sung the psalm and we have heard the gospel.' Later on in Rome a more elaborate scheme was worked out for the Saturdays of the Ember Weeks and for the Easter Vigil. Each reading was followed by a gradual (verses of a psalm) and a collect, the two latter reflecting the message of the reading.

The other element in the liturgy of the word was the Alleluia with its verses. St Jerome records that whenever a psalm had an Alleluia attached to it (as is frequently the case in the Hebrew) this was always sung, and it would seem that it was used at funerals (regarded as a celebration of the paschal mystery). He speaks of the sound of the people's voices echoing to the golden roof of the basilica.[5] He does not say, however, exactly at what point of the service it was sung, though it is certain that the Alleluia in both the East and the West was attached to the singing of the gospel. It was (and is) a preparation for the proclamation of Christ's word and accompanied the procession of the gospel book with deacon(s), lights and incense. In the West this rite was first adopted in Gaul, where the originally Greek acclamation, 'Glory to you, Lord' was used. This rite made its way to Rome in the seventh century. There, however, in the fifth century, the singing of the Alleluia was restricted to the Easter liturgy. Later it was extended to Easter time and by Gregory the Great to other parts of the year.

It should be noted that even in the liturgy of the word there was a distribution of roles and a certain hierarchical order. A lector, who at first did not need to be a cleric, read (or sang) the

[4] John Wilkinson, *Egeria's Travels* (S.P.C.K., 1971) pp. 55–56; 262–275.
[5] M. Righetti, *Manuale di Storia Liturgica* (Vol. III, 1949, Milan) p. 231.

Old Testament readings, a sub-deacon (until the Middle Ages regarded as in minor orders) read the epistle, and it was the prerogative of the deacon to sing the gospel.

Following on the readings came the homily, in which the president (either a bishop or a priest) broke the bread of God's word to the people, helping them to understand it and apply its message to their lives. Much of the literature of the Fathers of the Church, for example St Ambrose, St Augustine and St Leo in the West and St Gregory Nazianzos, St Cyril of Alexandria and St John Chrysostom in the East, consists of homilies that they preached at the liturgy.

The Prayer of the Faithful

This concluded the liturgy of the word, and is one of the most primitive elements of the eucharistic liturgy. Apart from the hint in I Timothy 2:2. there is in the letter of Pope Clement to the Corinthians of about the year 96 a long series of intercessions (though we do not know that they were actually used in a liturgical service), and, as we have seen, Justin and Hippolytus mention them. Other evidence can be gleaned from Tertullian at the end of the second century, from Cyprian in the middle of the third, and we have some information about them from Augustine in the fourth. They included petitions for rulers, for the state, for peace, for the lapsed, for catechumens and for the faithful generally.

In Rome the prayer had a particular form, the one with which we are familiar on Good Friday, called the Solemn Prayers. These almost certainly existed in the fourth century and, probably in the form of invitations to prayer and without the collects, in the third century. The collects are probably of late fourth century composition. All during the fifth century the Solemn Prayers were said at every Mass (private Masses were unknown) but by about the middle of the sixth century they had fallen out of use except for Good Friday and were replaced by a different kind of intercession.

It was held until recently that Pope Gelasius in the last decade of the fifth century introduced a litany-form of prayer with responses for the people, 'Hear, Lord, and have mercy' or something similar. That Gelasius wrote a litany called the *Deprecatio Gelasii* is certain, but after that disagreements among scholars

19

begin. The most recent view[6] is that his was not the first litany of its kind in the West and that similar litanies translated from eastern models had been making their way into the western liturgy for some time. Gelasius's, though it is described as a complete re-working of those models, was one among many. Secondly, it has been said that he ousted the Solemn Prayers and replaced them with his own litany. This almost certainly happened later. Thirdly, it has been said that he put his litany at the beginning of the Mass, but this is not certain. Somewhat later there *was* a litany at the beginning of the Mass in the 'title' or presbyteral churches of Rome, perhaps because the entrance psalm with all its solemnity was reserved to the papal Mass. Why the Solemn Prayers were replaced is a matter of speculation. The adult catechumenate was no longer in use in the sixth century, and there was no longer any need to have a dismissal after the homily. Everyone could be present for everything. Or it may be that the Solemn Prayers came to be regarded as unduly cumbersome and inflexible. One element the litany form of prayer introduced into the Roman rite was the threefold *Kyrie* which either preceded or followed the litany. As is clear from the eastern rites to this day it was regarded as a particularly urgent form of prayer, and Gregory the Great later on was to make much use of it.

The liturgy of the eucharist

The offertory

The first hints of an offertory are to be found in Hippolytus. At the ordination of a bishop the deacons are to present the 'offering' to him, and the catechumens are to bring nothing with them on the occasion of their initiation except their offering for the eucharist in which they will take part for the first time. Thirty or so years later, i.e. in the middle of the third century, it was common practice, for Cyprian rebukes a rich widow for bringing no offering, presuming, he said, to receive communion from the offerings brought by the poor. There was also an offertory towards the end of the fourth century in Africa and in Milan. St Augustine speaks of a procession and a chant accompanying it. There is no direct evidence for Rome at this time, but it seems likely that deacons received the people's offerings and placed what was not

[6] Paul de Clerk, *La 'Prière Universelle' dans les liturgies latines anciennes* (LQF, Band 62, 1977).

needed for the eucharist on splendid silver-plated tables that had been presented long before by Constantine. In the East and Southern Gaul (Arles) the people brought their offerings *before* the service. A similar custom was observed in the East and was the forerunner of the preparation rite (*proskomide*) in the Byzantine liturgy. In the West the preparation of the bread and wine before Mass was a feature of the Gallican rite. It survived until the end of the Middle Ages in, for example, the Sarum rite, and into modern times in the Dominican rite.

As will have been seen from the above there was a very close connection between the offering and holy communion; what was offered would, at holy communion, be returned, now changed into the Body and Blood of Christ. Each therefore must bring an offering and what was not needed for the eucharist was set aside and, with other things that had been brought, would be used for the support of the Church and the needy.

The appearance of the Roman Canon

The origins of the Roman Canon are not fully known. One or two quotations from it show that it existed in the middle of the fourth century but the first (apparently incomplete) text we have appears in certain catechetical instructions (*De Sacramentis*) to the newly-baptised by St Ambrose in the later years of the same century. Though, understandably, it differs in details from the Roman Canon, it is generally thought to be of Roman origin.[7]

It begins with the section that in our version comes immediately before the institution narrative: 'Grant to us that this offering may be approved, reasonable and acceptable ...' The words of institution are very similar to those of the Roman Canon, as is the *anamnesis*, recalling Christ's glorious passion, resurrection and ascension, and offering 'the spotless, reasonable[8] and bloodless victim'. There follows the prayer that the offering may be carried up to the heavenly altar by the hands of angels (in the plural) and there accepted by God as once he accepted the gifts of Abel, the sacrifice of Abraham and the offering made by Melchisedech.

The similarities of this text with the Roman Canon will be obvious, as also will certain omissions: the 'preface', the *Sanctus* and the next four sections are wanting. Did any of these sections

---

[7] For text in English translation see PEER, pp. 98–100.

[8] In the vocabulary of Ambrose 'reasonable' almost certainly means 'spiritual'; cf. Romans 12:1.

exist in the fourth century? Before giving the words of his canon Ambrose says that previously, 'Praise is offered to God, petition is made for the people, for kings and the rest'.[9] The 'praise' seems to refer to the 'preface', in which praise and thanks are given to God, and the 'prayer' seems to refer to that part of the canon where we pray for the Pope and the Church and for the offerers of the eucharist. But if this interpretation is not quite certain – and some scholars think the words refer to the Prayer of the Faithful before the canon – we have other texts that seem to support it. One, nearly contemporary, has a 'preface' and a petition for the acceptance of the sacrifice, and another, old but of uncertain date, has a prayer for the Church and for those who offer.[10] Further support can be gathered from a letter of 416 sent by Pope Innocent I to the Bishop of Gubbio, in which he speaks of the offerings that have been made and of those who have offered them. First, he says, the offerings are to be commended to God and then the names of the offerers are to be mentioned *inter sacra mysteria,* that is, within the canon and not in the 'prayers of the faithful' that precede it. What Innocent is speaking of is that section of the canon we call the Memento of the Living. This prayer then, or something very like it, was in use in Rome in the early fifth century, though not at Gubbio, where the older arrangement of naming the offerers *before* the eucharistic prayer still prevailed.

If we move back to the section of the Roman Canon that immediately follows the *Sanctus* there is evidence that it, too, existed in the fourth century, though in shorter form. There are echoes of it in a late fourth century canon, and in a phrase in the first of the ancient Solemn Prayers which asks that the Church may enjoy peace, unity and protection throughout the world, *'pacificare, adunare, custodire . . . toto orbe terrarum'*, words that still appear in the Roman Canon.

The rites of communion

In his description of the Mass, which is evidently incomplete, Ambrose does not mention the 'breaking of the bread', but it was in use everywhere. No ceremonies were as yet attached to it, and we gather from St John Chrysostom for the East and St Augustine

---

[9] Another translation is possible if the text is punctuated differently: '(There is) praise to God, prayer is offered and petition is made. . . .' The translation I have made seems to me the more probable.

[10] See PEER, pp. 101–103.

for the West that it was a purely utilitarian gesture: the bread was broken so that all might receive communion from it. In view of a change to be made later it is important to note that the breaking of the bread came at the end of the eucharistic prayer.

After the fraction came the Lord's Prayer, which is found in the eucharist at least from the beginning of the fourth century and perhaps earlier. As we have observed above, St Cyprian has a phrase that is close to the invitatory to the prayer as it still exists in our rite. It was certainly in the rite that Ambrose used: he comments on it at length in his instructions on the eucharist to the newly-baptised, but it may have been said after communion.

Ambrose does not attest the *pax,* or kiss of peace, but this, too, existed in his time, though everywhere in the Church except in Rome and North Africa it was exchanged *before* the eucharistic prayer began. For Rome, it is Innocent again who informs us that only 'after the mysteries have been completed' should the kiss of peace be given. Since only those who intended to receive communion were required to give the kiss of peace Innocent's rule may be evidence of the increasing infrequency of communion, about which St John Chrysostom at the same time complained in the East. In any case the Roman custom related the gesture to the words, 'forgive us our trespasses . . .'. When this change was made we do not know for certain, but it was probably towards the end of the fourth century.

Everyone who went to communion received it in both kinds. Ambrose again provides us with the formula: the celebrant said (as now in our rite), 'The Body of Christ' and the people replied, 'Amen'. There was a similar formula for the chalice. He also described how the newly-baptised come up to the altar, for he says that they are able to gaze on the sacred elements lying on it. In Africa, however, the people received communion at a position in front of the altar.

4.

The Completion of the Roman Rite: from Innocent I to Gregory the Great

Although the division of history by centuries is unsatisfactory – for history is a continuing process – the fifth century can be said to mark a great leap forward in the development of the liturgy. The catechumenate had achieved its classical form in the fourth century, and this was reflected in the liturgy of the eucharist. The catechumens were not allowed even to witness the enactment of the sacred mysteries and were dismissed (in the East with a blessing) after the liturgy of the word. This continued in Rome in the fifth century, though by the sixth century, when almost all had become Christians and infants were baptised, the catechumenate declined in importance. It was also the era of public penance. Those who sought reconciliation from the bishop and accepted the discipline of penance were excluded from holy communion, though in some places they were allowed to be present for the liturgy of the eucharist. These two practices conditioned the nature and length of the season of Lent, which in the fifth century was spread over a six (seven, in the East) week period before Easter.

It was at this time, too, that the main lines of the liturgical year appear. Beginning with Christmas (there was no Advent), it included Epiphany, Lent, Holy Week and Easter, the Fifty Days (the oldest part of the liturgical year), Ascension Day and Pentecost Sunday (the Fiftieth Day), which was rather the conclusion of Easter time than a special celebration of the Holy Spirit. This development, which emphasises the historical element, affected the liturgy of the Mass in various ways which can be seen in the variable prayers, in the readings and in the Canon itself. But before considering these it is necessary to deal with another practice that gave a new splendour to the liturgy.

The processional chants

In the oldest Roman tradition, as far as we can discern it, the Mass began with the first reading and without any other preliminaries.[1] Sometime in the fifth century an entrance chant, later called *Introit,* with a procession was added to the rite. Its origin seems to have been twofold. Under Constantine bishops were given senatorial rank, and in old pagan Rome when senators went on official business they were preceded by lighted torches and burning incense contained in a great vessel. On arrival at the senate house they were greeted in formal manner with chants. When therefore the Bishop of Rome went to celebrate the liturgy in one of the basilicas of the city a similar ceremonial was used and like the senators, it would seem, he was greeted with chants. Rather later evidence, however, suggests that there were differences. During the procession to the church there may have been a litany and the official chant of welcome was sung inside the church. This suggests the second reason for the chant. Long processions through a great church without song are dreary affairs and so the procession of the bishop from the *sacrarium* (sacristy) was accompanied by the singing of a psalm.

Already in Africa (and perhaps in Rome) in the late fourth century there was an offertory procession, accompanied by the chant called *offertorium*, when the people brought their offerings of bread and wine to the altar. This was parallelled by the communion procession when psalm 33, on account of the words 'Taste and see that the Lord is good', was often sung. These chants and their processions were not just ceremonial additions. They were functional, and the last two involved the whole assembly.

The variable prayers

These are the opening prayer, in Latin called *oratio* (and later the collect), the prayer over the offerings, and the postcommunion

[1] In Africa there was a preliminary greeting, 'The Lord be with you'.

25

prayer. The first, especially, reflected the theme of the liturgical season or feast, as it still does, and gives actuality to the celebration. Although the origin of these prayers remains obscure, it is probable that some of them at least existed before the time of Leo the Great (440–461), since he seems to quote from some of them in his sermons. There is also good reason to think that he composed some himself and that his style inspired others to do likewise. In any case a corpus of these prayers grew in the next two centuries or so, some identifiable as the work of subsequent popes. Short, succinct, with strong rhythmical patterns these prayers are generally regarded as among the finest texts of the Roman liturgy. Others, in freer style, were written in Spain and Gaul and in later centuries, but the classical Roman style declined after the seventh century.

These prayers were, like the processional chants, a functional addition to the liturgy. Then as now the opening prayer sums up the petitions of the people whom the president invites to pray, and on the great occasions of the liturgical year they turn into prayer the principal message of the day. The prayer over the offerings (for centuries the only one) brings the presentation of the gifts to a conclusion and forms the link with the eucharistic prayer. The Church prays that what the people have offered may be incorporated into the offering of Christ. The prayer after communion is not a 'thanksgiving' prayer but one that asks that the communicants may receive its fruits and express in their lives what they have received in the sacrament. For centuries it was the concluding text of the Roman Mass.

The course of readings

From the earliest times the only book used at the liturgy was the Bible, and this was in *codices* containing one or more books. Passages of the scriptures were read by an appointed reader and the president gave the sign when the reading should cease. There was a continuous reading of a book, though this was interrupted for the Easter liturgy and other important vigils when readings appropriate to the occasion were chosen. But the development of the liturgical year increased the number of occasions when this was so. Egeria, who was from the West, writing towards the end of the fourth century noted with some surprise and pleasure that in the Jerusalem liturgy the readings were adapted to times and places, the Holy Places. But, as we can gather from the sermons of this time, even in the West there were special readings for the great seasons and feasts of the year. In Holy Week certain readings from the gospel, says St Augustine, were chosen and the Passion according to Matthew was read on the sixth Sunday of Lent (later known as Palm Sunday). In Rome the gospel of the first Sunday of Lent was the Temptation of Christ, as it still is. The oldest Roman books show that the Passion according to John was read on Good Friday and this custom may go back to the sixth century. Luke 2 and Matthew 2 provided the readings for Christmas and Epiphany respectively. Augustine again attests that the Acts of the Apostles were read throughout Easter time (as they now are once again), as also the 'Catholic' epistles.

The earliest lectionaries, though of a later date, show that on the Sundays of the year (which were not yet fully organised) the epistles and gospels were read 'in course'. In general, then as now, the great phases of the history of salvation were unfolded in the liturgy. The Old Testament was regarded as a massive prophecy of the saving events of the New, as we can gather from the writings of many of the Fathers, and that is why the Old Testament was (and is) read in the course of liturgical celebrations.

As has been observed above, we cannot be sure that a psalm always followed the first reading or readings, but by the time of Augustine in Africa and Leo in Rome there was a psalm, sung by a cantor to a simple melody and replied to by the people with a response. These are the oldest chants of the rite and pre-date the processional chants.

The completion of the Roman Canon

The first known text of the completed Roman Canon is dated to the sixth century, some time before the reign of Gregory the Great. But it had been in process of formation since the fourth century, and we must now trace certain phases of that formation. First we must deal with the 'preface' and the *Sanctus*, and then with the rest of the Canon.

The 'Preface'

It will have been noticed that whenever this word has appeared, it has been put in inverted commas. This is because its nature has been, and still is, widely misunderstood. It is not a detached text, like the preface to a book. It is the first part of the eucharistic prayer, especially concerned with praise and thanksgiving. The *term* 'preface' has indeed been used in different senses at different times. St Cyprian, for instance, used it of the introductory dialogue (*Sursum corda* 'Lift up your hearts', etc.) to the eucharistic prayer, and in the fifth century and later it was used of various parts of the eucharistic prayer. One view, widely held, is that the word means a 'proclamation', a speaking out in the presence of someone. But this seems to be based on semantic considerations that are not necessarily applicable to the Christian Latin of the liturgy.

At first the term had the sense of a sacred and fixed formula. Hence Cyprian's use of it for the (then) one fixed text of the eucharistic prayer. Later it was used of different parts of the prayer. Furthermore, one or two early though fragmentary texts of the canon have no 'preface': in these the first part of the prayer, in which praise and thanksgiving are given to God, runs straight on, without the interruption of the *Sanctus,* into petition for the acceptance of the sacrifice. The true meaning of the term was later lost, and copyists began putting the word 'Canon' after the *Sanctus* so that the first part did in fact look like a preface. Unfortunately its meaning was further obscured when in the sacramentaries of the tenth and following centuries a large painting of the crucifixion was placed between the 'preface' and the rest of the Canon.[2]

The 'Sanctus' ('Holy, holy, holy Lord . . .')

That the *Sanctus* is a later addition to the eucharistic prayer can hardly be doubted. As we have seen, it is wanting in the prayer of Hippolytus, as in one or two late fourth century texts of the canon. Furthermore, there is a lack of continuity between the *Sanctus* and the *Te igitur,* which immediately follows. It is difficult to see what the '*igitur*' ('therefore') refers back to, though scholars have made various not very convincing suggestions about it. The Gallican and Spanish liturgists of the seventh and (probably) earlier centuries were aware of the gap and they provided a connecting phrase. Taking up the word 'holy' they wrote, 'You are indeed holy . . .', a phrase that is found in the new eucharistic

[2] Unhappily the error has been perpetuated by the printers of the *Missale Romanum* of 1970 who have put a picture and the words *Canon Romanus* after the *Sanctus.*

prayers II and III. Likewise in recent years the translators of the Roman Canon have felt the need to provide a connecting passage, and so we read, 'We come before you with praise and thanksgiving. . . .' The same problem presented itself to the authors of the fourth century eastern eucharistic prayers, for there are signs that the end of the first section had to be manipulated to make it lead into the *Sanctus.*

The *Sanctus* makes its first appearance in Alexandria in the middle of the fourth century and is found in the eucharistic prayer of Sarapion about 350. It seems to have made its way to the West thereafter. It was almost certainly in use in northern Italy, Aquileia, about the year 400, and in Ravenna (open to eastern influences) perhaps a little later. It was probably adopted in Rome shortly after 400. The *Liber Pontificalis,* a list of short biographies of the popes, attributes the inclusion of the *Sanctus* to Sixtus I (115–125), but there is good reason to think that this is a mistake for Sixtus III, who became pope in 432. In any case, we can be sure that the *Sanctus* was inserted into the Canon sometime between 417 and 432. As the *Liber Pontificalis* makes clear, it is the *people's* song, their response to the proclamation of the saving deeds of God they have just heard in the first part of the prayer. At first the text was much shorter, 'Holy, holy, holy Lord God of Sabaoth (hosts)'. This phrase was taken from Isaiah 6:3 (without the word 'God', which comes from the Latin translation and may witness to an eastern influence). The rest, which appears in the Gelasian Sacramentary, is from Isaiah 6:3, psalm 117 and Matthew 21:9.

In the previous chapter we have seen that, as well as the 'preface', the prayer for the Church and for those who offered formed part of the fourth century canon. Two sections, the *Communicantes* and the *Hanc igitur* were missing. These, and the sections after the institution-narrative have now to be investigated.

The 'Communicantes' ('In union with the whole church')

From a letter of Pope Vigilius (537–555) to Profuturus, Bishop of Braga (Portugal), we known that the *Communicantes* with its insertions for the great feasts already existed. Can we move back and find an earlier date for its existence? There are indications that it was a fifth century addition.

In all these earlier centuries the life of the Church is reflected in the liturgy. First there was the increasing devotion to Mary throughout the fourth century, given a new impulse by the Council of Ephesus (431), which declared her to be *Theotokos,* Mother of God. After the council Pope Sixtus III rebuilt and re-dedicated the basilica of St Mary Major, which to this day stands as a memorial of that council. It is thought, with good reason, that the insertion, 'We honour the ever-Virgin Mary, Mother of God (*Genetricis Dei*) and of our Lord Jesus Christ', was made at this time. This would indicate that the *Communicantes* already existed.

The addition of the names of the apostles and martyrs came in under a different influence. From the middle of the third century St Peter and St Paul had been honoured in Rome in a special way and, as the sermons of St Leo show, the feast of St Peter was a very great day there in the fifth century. Their names, then, and those of one or two more apostles, were included. There was also a growing sense of the importance of the martyrs, many of whom were popes, and so they also came to be included in this section of the Canon. It is in fact a very Roman list, most of them being local martyrs or those, like St Cyprian, with some special association with Rome. But for a long time the list remained flexible, and the strongly patterned form we now have in the Canon, with twelve martyrs corresponding to the twelve apostles, bears the marks of the hand of Gregory the Great (d. 604).

The third kind of insertion owes its existence to the developing liturgical year. There are five, covering the great feasts of the year, Christmas, Epiphany, Easter, the Ascension and Pentecost. We have sermons of St Leo for all these feasts and the insertions for Epiphany and the Ascension (as well as the prefaces) are very much in his style. It would seem safe to say, then, that these additions were being made in the middle of the fifth century, though there is no reason to suppose that they were complete until the time of Vigilius (d. 555). Anything like rigidity was not a characteristic of the Roman liturgy at this time. Gelasius is credited with the composition of '*praefationes*' and '*orationes*' (prayers) and we know that he composed a number of Mass-formularies. The purpose of these insertions seems to have been to actualise the eucharistic prayer, to help people to see that the mystery of salvation which is celebrated in every liturgy is rooted in the events of Christ's life, birth, passion, death and resurrection. In the late fifth century the Roman eucharistic prayer was becoming, or had become, the 'Canon', and some variation, as with the variable prayers, was regarded as necessary and desirable.

The 'Hanc igitur' ('Father accept this offering . . .')

Although the *Hanc igitur* would seem to be a still later addition than the *Communicantes,* it is convenient to consider it here. There are very numerous examples of it in the Verona book of the sixth century and from these it is possible to discern its original sense. It was a petition for the acceptance of the sacrifice on behalf of certain people, the newly-baptised, the newly-ordained and others. The first of these are still mentioned in the insertion for Easter Week. But the prayer was turned into a general petition for acceptance and the form in which it appears in the present text of the Canon was probably composed by Gregory the Great.

The 'Anamnesis' ('Father, we celebrate the memory of Christ, your Son . . .')

In the canon as we find it in St Ambrose only one prayer follows the institution narrative. In the Roman Canon, since the sixth century at least, this has been divided into two parts and a third section has been added. The first, the *anamnesis*, took up the words, 'As often as you do this, you do it *in memory* of me',[3] and expanded their meaning. Here we are at the heart of the eucharistic action. Jesus is no longer physically present to his Church but she, faithful to his command, recalls his passion, death, resurrection and ascension and by so doing makes sacramentally present and active among us the Christ who redeemed the human race. But further, now that our humble offering is identified with his, we can offer to the God of 'glory and majesty' this holy sacrifice, 'the bread of life and the cup of eternal salvation'.

The 'Supra quae' ('Look with favour on these offerings . . .')

The second prayer following the institution narrative is the *supra quae*. It is a prayer for the acceptance of the sacrifice: as God was once pleased to accept the gifts, offerings and sacrifice of Abel, Abraham and Melchisedech, so the Church asks that 'these offerings' may be accepted by him. This is a very ancient theme, found in the prayer of St Ambrose and represented in the sixth century mosaics above the altar in the church of St Vitalis at Ravenna. It is worth noting also that all these sacrifices pre-date

---

[3] Replaced in the Canon of 1970 by 'Do this in memory of me'.

those of the Temple and thus they may discreetly suggest the 'bloodless sacrifice' of the Mass.

To this prayer the words *sanctum sacrificium, immaculatam hostiam* ('the holy sacrifice and spotless victim . . .'—a phrase that has disappeared in our current translation) were added by Pope Leo I. It is strange that these weighty words should have been inserted as a kind of definition of Melchisedech's sacrifice, and they may originally have been attached to the end of the first prayer, '. . . the bread of life and the cup of salvation', or they may have been meant to apply to *all* that has gone before.

The 'Supplices te' ('Almighty God, we pray that your angel . . .')

This is an invocation, or *epiclesis,* though the Holy Spirit is not mentioned, that the sacrifice may be carried by an angel to the heavenly altar, with which the earthly altar is identified, so that all who receive communion *from the altar* may be 'filled with every grace and blessing'. If ever there was an invocation of the Holy Spirit in the Roman Canon (and Pope Gelasius seems to refer to one) it was here that it occurred.[4]

The Memento of the Dead and the following prayer

The general sense of these prayers is clear, and the Memento of

[4] The question is whether there was ever an *explicit* invocation of the Holy Spirit in the Roman Canon. The answer of scholars on the whole is in the negative, but some have pointed to certain texts, earlier than the Canon as we know it, that may suggest that there was. Ambrose, in his book on the Holy Spirit, speaks of him being invoked with the Father and the Son by the priests in baptism and 'in the offerings'. Gelasius, in a letter, asks, 'How shall the heavenly Spirit come if the priest who invokes him is stained by sinful actions?' There are other apparent references for North Africa in Optatus of Milevis (about 367) who speaks of the offering on the altar being sanctified by the Holy Spirit, and in St Augustine, who seems to echo him: 'It is only by the invisible operation of the Holy Spirit that (the eucharist) becomes holy and a great sacrament.' Finally, in the early years of the sixth century Fulgentius, a bishop in North Africa, speaks of the Holy Spirit coming to sanctify the sacrifice of the Church to preserve it in the union of love.

At a somewhat later date a sacramentary, written in France about the year 700, has an *epiclesis* invoking the Holy Spirit on the communicants.

However all that may be, even if there is no explicit *epiclesis* in the Roman Canon, it repeatedly asks for the acceptance of the sacrifice. In the prayer before the consecration the Church asks that the offering may be made acceptable and spiritual (*rationabilem*), and in the *Supplices* that those who receive the body and blood of Christ may be filled with 'heavenly blessing and grace' (compare with the 'heavenly Spirit' of the Gelasius text). And where blessing and grace are given, there is the action of the Holy Spirit.

the Dead occurs just where the intercessions come in the eastern eucharistic prayers. But there is a little puzzle connected with them. On Sundays and in the papal Masses in Rome the dead were not prayed for and the memento was omitted in spite of the fact that the following prayer is connected by an 'also'. But both appear in the oldest texts of the Canon and the first is certainly ancient, as is shown by its language. Those who have gone before us are 'marked with the sign of faith', that is, baptism, and the prayer asks that they may be received into a place called *refrigerium,* a place of refreshment and happiness. Because it was not used in papal Masses the memento disappeared from some manuscripts, but gradually, and especially outside Rome, it came into use for all Masses. In Ireland the deacon read out the names of the dead.

A curious text

Many have remarked on the prayer that follows, where we ask that God may hallow, enliven and bless the gifts he has created. Do these words apply to the eucharist? The answer is No. At this point in the Canon on certain occasions gifts, presented by the people (including oil for the anointing of the sick), were blessed by the presiding bishop. In the eucharistic prayer of Hippolytus they were blessed immediately after the doxology, which is probably the original place for the action.

The doxology

All eucharistic prayers end with a more or less elaborate doxology in which there is an ascription of 'glory and honour' to the Father, through the Son in the Holy Spirit. The Trinitarian pattern of the eucharistic prayer is thus summed up and brought to its highest point of expression. Since the days of St Justin the people have always given their assent to the whole of the preceding eucharistic action by their Amen.

The revision of the Roman Canon

As well as the completion of the Roman Canon there was a certain rewriting of it somewhere between 450 and 550 in the now developed Latin of the papal *curia.* Observable in papal letters, it is a style that is balanced and elegant, and is easily detectable in the rhythmical phrases that occur throughout the prayer. Thus in the section after the *Sanctus* we find *haec dona, haec munera, haec sancta sacrificia illibata* ('These gifts, these offerings, these holy and spotless sacrifices'), which has a distinctly rhetorical cadence. Or again, immediately following we have the words *pacificare, custodire, adunare et regere*, used of the Church, in which God is asked to give peace to it, to guard it, and unite and govern it. An almost identical phrase is found in the first of the Solemn Prayers of Good Friday which, as we have seen, belong to the late fourth century. This, and the addition of Pope Leo's *sanctum sacrificium, immaculatam hostiam,* may give a clue to the time when the revision was made.

The formation of the liturgical books

Until recently it was not easy to see that the missal was a composite book made up of four or five others. Since the liturgical reform we have become accustomed to the notion that the Mass requires at least two books: the lectionary, and the missal containing all the texts needed by the celebrant. This is in fact a partial return to an earlier tradition and if we are to understand the next stage of liturgical development we must consider the formation of the liturgical books from which the missal was eventually compiled.

In the fifth century there was no one book containing all the texts necessary for the Mass, much less one with all the texts to be used throughout the year. Prayers were composed and written out for each occasion on parchments which contained the opening, offertory and post-communion prayers and one of the variable prefaces, very numerous in the sixth century. These booklets were called *libelli* and, after use, were filed in the Lateran or elsewhere so that they could be taken out and used on some future occasion. The celebrant made his choice from the sometimes very numerous Mass-formularies that were available. The *libelli* were later collected into books which were called sacramentaries, since they contained the essential texts for the celebration of the sacrament of the eucharist.

The oldest collection (sixth century) was for long called the 'Leonine Sacramentary', though it is neither Leonine nor a sacramentary. It was called 'Leonine' because its first editors thought that many of the prayers had been written by St Leo. There are in fact texts in it that date from his time, but there are also many later ones. It is not a sacramentary because its arrangement is haphazard and disorderly, so that it is quite useless for celebration. However, it is still of great interest since it contains many prayers that are still to be found in the Roman Missal. It is now usually called the Verona Sacramentary because the MS. was discovered in the Chapter Library of the Cathedral at Verona.

The first sacramentary properly so-called is the Gelasian (though Gelasius had nothing to do with it) and is of the late seventh century, though containing older elements. Apparently produced in the same way as the Verona book, it is well organised in three parts: the first covering the great seasons and feasts of the year, the second giving the Mass-formularies for saints' feasts, and the third containing prayers and other texts for a great variety of occasions. This last section includes the Roman Canon, with the interesting rubric *before* the dialogue and the preface: *Incipit Canon Actionis* ('Here begins the Canon of the (eucharistic) Action'). It was compiled and probably written (at least in part) by the clergy of the parish churches of Rome (the 'Tituli', or titular churches, much later assigned to cardinals). Since it was intended for the use of the presbyters (priests) of these churches all the year round it has a great deal more material than the 'Gregorian Sacramentary' which was used only for the papal liturgy. Either as a whole or in sheafs (*libelli*) it made its way into France in the seventh century, where a second 'edition' incorporating elements from the Gallican books, and even from the Gregorian Sacramentary, appeared, known as the 'Eighth Century Gelasian'. The fusion of the Gelasian, in both forms, with the Gregorian is the basis of the Roman Missal.

The Gregorian Sacramentary has long borne the name of the saint, but his part in its compilation is not easy to discern. That he wrote prayers, revised others and composed some texts (e.g. the Preface of Christmas) seems certain, and in this sense he was but continuing the work of his predecessors. But it is much less certain that he was the compiler of the whole collection. There are feasts in it (including his own!) that post-date his death and other additions were made in the latter part of the seventh century, when the book is thought to have reached completion. But Gregory's name became attached to it and accordingly it acquired immense prestige. It must be emphasised that it was a book for *papal* services and since these were limited to the great seasons and feasts of the year it makes no provision for the Sundays of the year, and this material had to be supplied later from the Gelasian and other sources. Like the Gelasian it existed in various 'editions', mostly made in France, and of neither of these books have we a copy in its original state. In conclusion it may be remarked that it was in use at the same time as the Gelasian, which shows that liturgical uniformity even in Rome was not insisted on.

Of the lectionary we have said a little above, and a word must be spared for the song-books without which the liturgy could not be celebrated. The *Cantatorium* contained the texts of the psalms to be sung between the readings and was later combined with the processional chants in a book which came to be called the *Graduale* (from the *gradus*, or step, from which the cantor sang the psalm). As with the sacramentary, so with the chant book or books Gregory's part in their revision is very uncertain. A *schola cantorum,* a school for singers, developed in the seventh century, as did the chant itself, though until the tenth century all the melodies had to be learnt by heart as they were not written down.

The *Ordines Romani,* the oldest of which is of the seventh century, were books giving instructions on how the liturgical services, at first only papal services, were to be organised. The papal Mass was a very elaborate affair involving many clerics and the whole court, and directives were necessary. The *Ordines* were compiled over a number of centuries, the last being of the four-teenth century (when the papacy was at Avignon) in which the necessary adaptations to conditions north of the Alps were made for the celebration of the liturgy. The first, the *Ordo Romanus Primus,* which gives a description of the papal Mass in the seventh century, is of considerable interest for there we can discern the main structure of the (High) Mass as it was known until the reforms of the Second Vatican Council. The rubrics of the Pius V missal of 1570 and the General Instruction of the Roman Missal of 1970 are the successors of the *Ordines Romani.*

St Gregory the Great and the liturgy

Since the eighth century Gregory's name has been associated with a reform of the liturgy but his work in it is, as has been said, difficult to discern. The Roman Canon had by now become fixed: the first text we have dates from his time (590–604). He revised some of the prayers in the sacramentary called after him and made three changes in the Order of the Mass.

The first of these concerns the Prayer of the Faithful. This, in litany-form, had continued in use but Gregory made three changes:

(1) 'Those things it is customary to say' (i.e. the litany) were dropped on week-days;
(2) they were replaced by the singing of the *Kyrie* alternated between the clerics and the people;
(3) unlike the Greeks, from whom Gregory was accused of adopting this custom, in Rome *Christe eleison* was sung and as many times as the *Kyrie*.

The custom of singing a threefold *Kyrie* at the beginning of the litany was almost certainly in use before Gregory's time so he could plead that he had not adopted it directly from the Greeks. It was regarded as a particularly urgent form of prayer and Gregory liked to dwell on it. After his time the intercessions were dropped altogether[5] and thus the people were deprived of expressing their needs in the course of the Mass. The *Kyrie* with *Christe* has however remained in the rite though its position is somewhat anomalous.

The second change was to make the *Hanc igitur* a fixed text with a single petition (except at Easter and Pentecost): 'Father, accept this offering ... *Grant us your peace in this life, save us from eternal damnation and count us among those you have chosen*' – which is quite in the style of St Gregory.

The third change was more radical. Gregory moved the breaking of the bread from its place at the end of the Canon and put the Lord's Prayer there. The reason for this seems to have been that in papal ceremonial the pope received holy communion at his chair behind the altar where, as part of the communion rite, the Lord's Prayer had formerly been said. He wished to say it at the altar, and so moved it to the end of the eucharistic prayer. There it remains to this day. The change had unfortunate consequences. The prayer did not now appear so clearly as a prayer of preparation for communion and the significance of the third great action of the eucharist, the breaking of the bread, became obscured. This, which originally always took place at the end of the eucharistic prayer, was moved further away from the institution narrative, and when, later on, the action became embedded in a mass of

[5] They continued to be used in Gaul for some time.

ceremonial at the end of the embolism it was hardly noticed at all. In spite of the recent revision the 'breaking' is not as prominent as it should be. It would however be more significant if celebrants did what the General Instruction (n. 283) urges them to do, viz. to use a larger altar-bread so that it can be seen to be broken up and at least some of the people can receive communion from it.

The Lord's Prayer is followed by an insertion (an *embolism*) which probably existed in the fourth century in shorter form, but the text was rewritten and it is thought that Gregory is responsible for the version that existed in our missals until 1970.

The papal Mass in the seventh century

We are fortunate in having a document (*Ordo Romanus Primus*) which enables us to see what the papal Mass was like in the seventh century. Though long, it is necessary to give some account of it as it exercised an enduring influence on the subsequent history of the Mass.

The celebrant is the pope who is going to celebrate a stational Mass, i.e. one previously appointed, on a great feast. Preceded by the seven deacons of Rome, their subdeacons, and seven acolytes carrying lighted candles, and followed by members of the papal court, he goes to the appointed church. After being vested in the sacristy he gives a sign with his *mappa* (later, maniple) for the procession and the entrance psalm to begin. This accompanies the procession to the altar until the pope gives the sign for the singing to cease. After reverencing the altar and greeting the clergy he prays briefly in silence. During these actions the *schola* (the choir) sing the *Kyries*. If it is Christmas or Easter the pope intones the *Gloria in excelsis* – a privilege long reserved to these feasts and, in fact, to the pope and to bishops. He then greets the people with *Pax vobiscum* (Peace be to you), as a bishop does today, and sings the opening prayer.

The liturgy of the word follows, the epistle being sung by a subdeacon and the gospel by a deacon who, after a blessing from the pope, goes in solemn procession to the ambo, preceded by two acolytes with lighted candles and accompanied by two subdeacons, one carrying a thurible.

Immediately after this the altar is prepared. It is covered with a single cloth and then a chalice is brought, on which is a large corporal which two deacons unfold. In the rite of the offertory that follows it should be noted that it is the pope and his ministers who move, not the people. The whole action was quite complicated but when over the pope sang the (single) prayer over the offerings. The Canon follows, pronounced aloud (probably sung), so that all could hear it, including the words of consecration. There is no elevation, but at the end of the Canon the archdeacon raises the chalice and the pope touches it with the consecrated bread. He now sings the Lord's Prayer and gives the kiss of peace to his ministers and the people exchange it among themselves. The pope then goes to his chair and there begins the long ceremony of the breaking of the bread, each bishop and priest breaking his own. Meanwhile the *Agnus Dei* (inserted by Pope Sergius I, d. 701) is sung, and only then does the pope receive communion. He then communicates the notables, and other ministers the rest of the people.

The Mass ends with the prayer after communion and the dismissal sung by the archdeacon: *Ite, missa est* (Go, the Mass is finished).

5.

The Propagation of the Roman Rite: from Charlemagne to Innocent III

With the decline of the Roman Empire in the West in the eighth century the balance of power passed to the new countries that were forming north of the Alps. The centre of liturgical interest also passed to that area.

England and the Roman rite

Under the impact of the invasions of various tribes from Germany the Church in Britain, which was organised if small in the fourth century, died out except in Wales and perhaps Cornwall. During the sixth century northern England was evangelised by Irish monks from Iona in Scotland and in 597 St Augustine, sent by St Gregory, landed in the South to begin the work of conversion there. Whether or not he brought with him the Gregorian Sacramentary (and most probably he did not), he brought whatever books were necessary for the celebration of the liturgy. For the Mass this will have been an 'edition' of a pre-Gregorian sacramentary. In the next century the North was 'Romanised' by St Wilfrid, who at the decisive Synod of Whitby in 664 persuaded the King to adopt Roman liturgical use, and by his contemporary Benet Biscop, who brought back from Rome quantities of books, both liturgical and other, when he was founding the monasteries of Monkwearmouth and Jarrow. The whole process was completed in the eighth century when the Synod of Clovesho in 747 decreed that the Roman rite should be used throughout the land. England was thus the first country outside Rome to adopt the Roman rite.

The Carolingian reform

A few years later the Church in Frankish lands (roughly, France and West Germany) underwent a revival, first thanks to Pepin III (714–768) and secondly to the English monk, Boniface, the apostle of Germany, who ably assisted him in his task.

From at least the fifth century the old Roman provinces in the south of France had had a liturgy of their own with one or two ancient and even Greek features. It is known as the Gallican liturgy. But from the same century onwards successive invasions of barbarians from the East and again the Moslem invasion in the eighth century had devastated the land and disorganised the Church. Churches and monasteries were destroyed and their contents scattered. The copying of the necessary liturgical books had become impossible and the ancient Gallican liturgy was in a state of chaos. Liturgical celebrations not only differed from diocese to diocese but from church to church. Moreover there was no great centre, whether cathedral or monastery, to which men might look for reform. On the other hand the prestige of the Roman Church had been steadily increasing throughout the seventh century and Gallic ecclesiastics had sought books there for use in the liturgy at home. During the reign of Pepin relations with Rome were particularly close – he had rescued the Pope from the domination of the Lombards – and it was in these circumstances that he looked to Rome for help to begin the moral and liturgical revival of his lands. Metz, where Chrodegang, his relative, had established a chapter of canons living according to a rule, became a centre of the Roman chant based on a responsorial and an antiphoner which Pepin had obtained in Rome. Pepin's success was real, though limited, and his work was to be completed by his son Charlemagne.

During the first years of his reign Charlemagne was occupied with the conquest of vast territories in what is now Germany, when he 'converted' multitudes of people at the point of the sword. Once he had established his empire he turned, among other things, to the organisation of the liturgy. Chaos was to give place to uniformity, and throughout his realm there was to be but one liturgy. But the centre of unity was Rome, ruled at this time by a great pope, Hadrian I (d. 795). Sometime before 790 he sent him a request for an authentic copy of the Roman Sacramentary. This, after some delay (for there seems to have been a shortage of books in Rome too), he duly received. This was the Gregorian Sacramentary, not in its primitive form (of which no copy is extant), but with the accretions of the seventh and eighth centuries. It is known as the (*Sacramentarium*) *Hadrianum*. When Charlemagne's advisers looked into the book they found, no doubt to their dismay, that there was much wanting in it, as well as much (from the family of liturgical books known as the Eighth Century Gelasian) with which they were already familiar. In short, it was a book arranged for papal celebrations which took place only in the greater seasons and on the greater feasts of the year.

It had, then, to be adapted to the needs of the Church north of the Alps, and this is how it was done. The *Hadrianum* was left intact and an editor added a supplement that included texts for the Sundays of the year, the *Exultet* for the Easter Vigil (not used in the papal rite), and a collection of Masses for various saints' feasts, for various occasions and 'votive Masses'. Thus came into being the book that was to survive, to all intents and purposes, as the book of the Roman Mass for centuries to come.

Who was the editor? It is a question of some interest to English people. Until recently it was thought to have been the English monk, Alcuin of York, whom Charlemagne met in Italy and invited to his court at Aachen to assist him in his educational programme. But recent investigations have pointed in the direction of the great monastic reformer, Benedict of Aniane, who was also associated with the work of the palace school. Alcuin had left the court some years before he died in 804 and the first Carolingian edition of the *Hadrianum* (without the Supplement) is now dated to the years between 810 and 815. Benedict died in 821. Furthermore, the Latin of the introduction to the Supplement does not seem to be Alcuin's, and certain texts with Spanish features are more credibly attributed to Benedict, who lived near the Spanish border. Present opinion, then, is that it was Benedict who compiled the Supplement, which began with the word *Hucusque*: '*Up to this point* the book is a copy of the *Hadrianum* and the rest is from other sources'.[1] Unfortunately, later copyists omitted the careful instruction of the editor and the two books became

[1] Jean Deshusses, *Le sacramentaire grégorien* I (1971); II (1979); Fribourg, Switzerland. A third volume has yet to appear.

42

fused, so that for centuries no one realised that the Roman Missal was itself an amalgam.

What then of the contribution of Alcuin? He certainly edited a lectionary of the Mass, and opinion is firmly in favour of his having written the section of 'votive Masses', among which we find the formulary for the Feast of Holy Trinity, parts of which we still use. He also composed Masses for certain saints' feasts and re-wrote the prayers we still use for the Feast of All Saints which he did much to propagate.

As yet, however, we are far away from the Roman Missal and liturgical uniformity. The new edition of the Roman book, with all its additions, remained a sacramentary containing only those texts needed by the celebrant. The lectionaries and the song-books remained separate and were used by the appropriate ministers and singers. For the model of the liturgy was still the High Mass, based on the *Ordo Romanus Primus*, adapted to the circumstances that prevailed in Charlemagne's empire. The emperor did much by synods and legislation from 789 to 805 to raise liturgical standards. He insisted that the people should sing the *Sanctus,* the *Kyries* and one or two other texts – perhaps because he was a layman and did not want to remain silent throughout the Mass! But the fact that he had to legislate for more than sixteen years shows that he achieved what he did only with difficulty. The contemporary equivalent of 'new-fangled' was no doubt heard often enough. Furthermore, the notion of uniformity in liturgy was too new to be accepted (the Gelasian books continued to be used) and it was never achieved throughout the Middle Ages. Yet Charlemagne established a model, and in all the bewildering changes of the coming centuries the core of the Roman rite remained intact.

The obscuring of the pattern

The Roman liturgy had now moved into a different civilisation with different psychological attitudes and different needs. These were to make their impact on the rite.

Early on there were one or two enrichments of the liturgy: the addition of the *Exultet* for Easter Eve has been mentioned above, and the rite of Palm Sunday with its processions and chants appears for the first time in the Romano-German Pontifical of the tenth century. But other additions and changes that were now made did much to obscure the basic pattern of the Roman rite.

Under the influence of Spain, where Arianism (which denied the divinity of Christ) was prevalent, new prayers were composed addressed to Christ rather than to the Father. Christ's role as mediator between God and man, central to the eucharist, was somewhat diminished. Moreover, the Roman liturgy seemed too austere for the more ebullient and emotional temperaments of northern Europe. Hence from the ninth century onwards a whole corpus of individualistic prayers was introduced into the liturgy, first as private devotions which a celebrant might say while he was not required to say the official texts, and then as quasi-official texts attached to the rite. There were interpolations even in the *Sanctus* and the Canon of the Mass. Because these prayers protested the unworthiness of the celebrant they were known as *apologiae*. The trend towards making the celebration of the Mass a private devotion of the celebrant was already on its way.

The eucharist is a celebration for a community by a community, and this aspect of it tended to disappear. As early as the seventh century the people's chants had been taken over by the clergy, and then the *schola* took them over from the clergy. Greater emphasis was now put on the president (bishop or priest) and his ministers, and the people were regarded more and more as recipients and observers of what they did. In Rome and Italy Latin could still be understood by the people in a general way but north of the Alps it was a totally foreign language, known only to clerics. Notions of awe and of ritualistic purity (there were strict rules for married people, who must receive communion in a state of continence) and primitive sentiments about guilt contributed to an ever less frequent reception of communion. Also, perhaps on account of the crude manners of the barbarian converts and for reasons of reverence, communion from the chalice became rare, though infants were still communicated from it after baptism and the custom did not die out until the later Middle Ages. The old offertory procession had died out (except for funerals and one or two other occasions) and the link between the people's offering and communion was broken. An ominous mark of this was the insertion in the Canon in the ninth century of the words at the Memento of the Living, '*for* whom we offer'. During this same period the communion bread underwent a change of content and form. It now became unleavened (i.e. doughless) bread, and the particles for the people became small, round and white. There was now nothing to break before communion except the celebrant's 'host'. The *Agnus Dei* thus became a communion chant. Finally, the Canon, which had been sung or proclaimed in a loud voice, now became silent and so the principal part of the Mass was no longer heard by the people.

Another development witnesses to both the increasing clericalisation and monasticism of the Church. There was an ever-increasing reverence for saints' relics and these, in caskets, began to be placed on the altar or above it. The *actions* of the celebrant were now obscured, and when a new wave of monasticism spread over Europe – in itself a sign of the renewal of the Church – the arrangement of the sanctuary underwent a change. Monks, nuns and regular canons were committed to the singing of the Divine Office eight times a day. In the winter churches were cold and so 'choirs' were built with stalls and canopies over them to keep out at least some of the draught. The altar, which impeded the movement of the choir, was placed nearer to the East wall until in the end it was attached to it. Then towards the end of the tenth century a cross (only later a crucifix) was put on the altar and finally the candlesticks, seven for a bishop (derived from the papal liturgy) and six for anyone else! When certain architectural arrangements came to be made, especially in the Gothic period, namely when there were to all intents and purposes two churches under one roof, the choir for the monks or canons and the nave, the division between the clergy and the laity became even more marked.

However, the austerity of the rite and its unintelligibility (at least for the people) were somewhat compensated for by mural pictures, by stained-glass windows which told the story of salvation, and by an increasing dramatisation of the liturgy. In cathedrals and monastic churches there was an enactment of the resurrection. On Good Friday a cross (and later a consecrated host) was 'buried' in a sepulchre and deacons and other clerics on Easter morning in dramatic fashion 'searched' for it and brought it back with song to the high altar. The Palm Sunday procession became ever more elaborate and often included a donkey on which the celebrant rode into church. These and other practices (not always free from abuses) gave rise to the passion and morality plays of the later Middle Ages.

Meanwhile another development was taking place. The 'Gregorian' chant, whose origins are very remote, was more and more elaborated in the Roman *schola* and the monasteries. This affected in particular the Alleuias before the gospel, the last syllable being endowed with a great number of notes. The Roman and monastic singers could no doubt cope with this difficult form of melody, which was not written down until the tenth century and then only in a sort of code, but other singers found it difficult. They therefore inserted words into the melodies and out of these grew the 'sequences' (something that 'follows'). The oldest appears to be the *Victimae paschali* for Easter. The *Veni Sancte* for Whitsunday is attributed to Stephen Langton, Cardinal-Archbishop of Canterbury (d. 1228) and the *Lauda Sion* for Corpus Christi (1264) to St Thomas Aquinas (d. 1274). This, as is known, is very long and, like the *Dies irae* (an Advent and not a funeral hymn) and the *Stabat Mater* (inserted into the Mass only in the eighteenth century), does not fit easily into the liturgy.

The German intervention

The centre of political power had moved again, this time from France to Germany. The new Capetian monarchy was only slowly establishing itself in France and the papacy had fallen into the hands of the robber-barons in and around Rome. The need to restore order was acute, and this, at the cost of the independence of the papacy, the German Emperors (called 'Holy, Roman', though they were not Roman and rarely holy) achieved in the eleventh century.

Meanwhile there had been liturgical activity in the Rhineland, and it is there that we find the first outline of an Order of the Mass that had a long history before it. For the first time we find the antiphon 'I will go to the altar of God' with psalm 42 followed by avowals of sinfulness, certain prayers of a Spanish type ('Accept, holy Trinity . . .'), the prayer for the mixing of the chalice (which still exists in our rite in an earlier form), the prayers to be said at the incensation of the altar (done only at the offertory), certain prayers (usually from Gallican sources) which overlaid the Canon and three prayers (for the priest) before communion, two of which remain in the Order of 1970. But the rite envisaged was a High Mass and these additions remained unperceived by the people. They were *unofficial* prayers intended for the private devotion of the celebrant, though the unwary and uninstructed priest did not always see this. When the emperors, the Ottonians and their successors, 'liberated' Rome and the papacy it was this book together with the Romano-German

Pontifical (with its anointings for the ordination of bishops and priests) that they brought with them. One of them, Henry II, when he came to Rome in 1014 to be crowned emperor insisted that the Creed should be inserted into the Mass. Originally an element of the baptismal rite, it had been used at Mass in Spain (as well as in the East) for some long time and since the eighth century also in the Frankish empire. Roman, Gallican, Spanish and now German elements thus constituted what was thought to be the Roman rite which one day would be imposed on the whole of the Latin church.

This Order of the Mass could be said to foreshadow the full missal, called the *Missale plenum*, in which all the texts of the rite, chants, readings, prayers and the Canon were assembled in one book. Since the seventh century, when monks were regularly ordained priests, the practice of private Masses in small chapels had been growing. Every monk wished to say Mass if not daily then very frequently, and no doubt the priest in a rural area could not possibly have had all the books necessary for the celebration of the Mass. By the twelfth century the *Missale plenum* was in general use, though differing considerably in detail (different sets of private prayers) from one region to another. But unhappily, since the priest now had everything in one book he tended to say everything he found there, so that there grew up a confusion of roles. The parts of the reader and the singers gradually became absorbed by the celebrant, and in the sixteenth century it became a matter of law that he should say whatever was said or sung by anyone else. The rite of what came to be called Low Mass thus invaded – and further distorted – the pattern of the rite. Even in the Middle Ages the discrepancy between what the priest was saying privately and what was happening publicly was remarked upon.

With the coming of Pope Gregory VII (d. 1085), who finally freed the papacy from the domination of the German Emperors, there began a period of redressment. Discipline was tightened up, there was a centralisation of power in Rome, and some cleaning up of the liturgy. Gregory disliked certain contributions of the 'Teutons' and rejected them, but most of the unofficial additions to the Mass remained. The old Roman papal liturgy was again celebrated with splendour, but as the popes got more and more busy so the papal court (the *curia*) developed. To provide for their and the pope's spiritual and liturgical needs a papal chapel was established in the Lateran. It was very splendid, filled with relics and glittering with gold. But the liturgy had perforce to be somewhat truncated. The officials of the court were very busy and could not be expected to have the expertise of trained singers. The papal chapel, then, developed its own style of liturgy which was used alongside that of the Lateran Basilica and indeed that of St Peter's, whose liturgy differed in some details from the Lateran's. Strict uniformity, even in Rome, was as yet unknown.

The 'German' Order of the Mass in essence survived all these changes and the Order or Ordinal of the papal chapel that developed in the twelfth century was very like it. Its main constituents can be gathered from a somewhat allegorical commentary on the Mass written by Innocent III (1198–1216) before he became pope. He mentions psalm 42 and the confession, but the Order of the papal court a little later makes clear that the priest is to say the psalm on his way to the altar. Innocent remarks, however, that while the celebrant is saying the confession and incensing the altar with *its* prayers the entrance chant is being sung. Nor had all 'German' additions been welcome: there are no prayers at the offertory.[2]

In twelfth century Rome there were several Orders of the Mass in use, differing from each other in details, and the relation of one to another is complicated. But sometime before 1227, in the reign of Honorius III, an Order appeared with the sub-title 'according to the Use of the Roman Church', i.e. court. This, if anything, is the predecessor of the Order of the Roman Missal of 1570. A few observations are in place. The psalm and its antiphon are still said on the way to the altar, though the confession is included, to be said during the singing of the entrance chant: that is, it was a private devotion. The six prayers (again private) to be said at the offertory, as in the missal of 1570, appear for the first time, and there are nine prefaces, though another Order, perhaps a little earlier, gives eleven, including the Preface of the Cross, given only as a 'votive' preface in the Honorius Order. There are also the three prayers for the priest's devotion before communion together with the 'Lord, I am not worthy', again intended for the priest and not the people. The Mass ends with the dismissal.

<hr>

[2] Innocent is the first (after the Augustinians in Jerusalem) to mention a series of liturgical colours: purple, white, scarlet and 'hyacinth' (violet?). Originally *black* was the penitential colour in Rome.

There is no blessing.[3]

It was this book, with a few minor changes, that the newly-founded Franciscans took with them all over Europe and beyond. The rite envisaged in it is indeed the High Mass, but it had to be adapted to different circumstances prevailing outside Rome if it was to be used for Low Mass. Because it bore the sub-title 'according to the Use of the Roman Church' it gained a certain prestige and came to be used even by those who were not Franciscans. But it was never imposed as an official rite and local rites and those belonging to religious orders continued to be used until 1570.

The elevation

Nor was there uniformity in the books that derived from the papal Order. The number and even the text of prayers (e.g. at the offertory) varied from one book to another and there was a great variety of local customs within the rite. The Franciscan missal, for instance, was edited in the middle of the thirteenth century by an Englishman, Haymo of Faversham, and differed in a few details from the Roman book. One example of the differences is the elevation of the host after the consecration. This custom had been introduced in the early years of the thirteenth century and was approved by a Bishop of Paris about the year 1208. But until 1282 the Franciscans were *forbidden* to elevate the host. Perhaps they regarded it as a new-fangled French custom, as indeed it was. However, the custom spread rapidly throughout Europe, and is found first in the Roman Order of 1227, though the elevation of the chalice became general only towards the end of the century. The practice of elevating the host soon became very popular (it was in use in London by 1215), and as people received communion ever less frequently so their 'desire to see the host' increased. In England, a little later, we have the story of the devout worshipper who cried out to the priest who did not raise the host high enough for him to see it, 'Heave it higher, Sir John, heave it higher'. If the gesture was helpful to the devotion of a people who had little enough participation in the Mass, it threw the emphasis on but one moment of the eucharistic celebration to the detriment of

[3] S. J. P. Van Dijk, *The Ordinal of the Papal Court from Innocent III to Boniface VIII and Related Documents;* completed by Joan Hazelden Walker (Fribourg, Switzerland, 1975).

others. This imbalance had been corrected by the General Instruction of the Roman Missal of 1970, which states: 'The Eucharistic *Prayer* . . . is the climax and very heart of the entire celebration' of the Mass (n. 54).

In the same period signs of the cross and other gestures during the Canon were greatly multiplied, concealing rather than revealing its true pattern. In the Canon of the Gelasian Sacramentary there are but five signs of the cross, probably meant to be gestures pointing to the offerings. In the Canon of the 1570 missal there are twenty-five.

6.

The Later Middle Ages

Although with hindsight we can we see that the Order of the Mass according to the use of the Roman court marked the beginning of liturgical uniformity, the situation in Europe remained what it was. If the Mozarabic rite of Spain was languishing, the ancient rite of Milan continued to flourish. Alongside these there were many variations within the Roman rite that are best called 'Uses'. These were customs, both national and regional, that had become attached to the basic Roman rite. Paris and Rouen, for instance, had theirs, and England had no less than five, of which that of Sarum (Salisbury) was the best known and most widely used. Some of these 'uses' were of considerable beauty, that of Sarum being marked by much movement and a joyful spirit, expressive of the medieval English temperament. The religious orders, the Carthusians (very austere – there was no elevation of the chalice), the Carmelites, the Dominicans, the Premonstratensian Canons, all had their own 'rites'. A medieval Catholic going to a Dominican church one Sunday and a Franciscan church the next would have found certain differences, but they probably did not disturb him very much. But it is important to understand that all these 'rites' were those of communities, whether regional, diocesan or religious; they did not belong to private groups who wanted to 'do their own thing'.

But the situation was very untidy. Liturgical books, still written by hand, differed in text and in the number of prayers from one region to another and even from one book to another. Apart from the great seasons and feasts, the local calendars became filled up with (local) saints' feasts, several occurring on the same day, all

51

of which had to be commemorated in collects and the corresponding prayers, seven being the highest number allowed in a single Mass or Office. The priest celebrated with his back to the people, often in churches that were quite dark, all was in Latin and the scripture readings passed unnoticed. The Canon was silent and in sung Masses overlaid by the *Sanctus,* sung to increasingly more elaborate music. Communion was still infrequent, and everything seemed to be of the same importance – or unimportance – except perhaps for the elevation of the host and chalice. Although there was a sense of community in the country parishes – and most of Europe was still rural – it was difficult to express it in the liturgy.

There was however at least one popular feature of the rite. This was what was called in England the Bidding Prayers, which were mostly in the vernacular. They included very long 'biddings', i.e. invitations to prayer, for the pope, the bishop, the monarch, the local Church, and the sick and the dead, for whom the psalm *De profundis* was recited. In addition, the Lord's Prayer and the Hail Mary (the first part only) punctuated the biddings. In the Sarum rite they were very long, but as there was rarely a sermon at Mass – the new mendicant orders, the Franciscans, the Dominicans and the rest had practically monopolised preaching, which took place outside the Mass – this was no great hardship. The parish priest often added injunctions from the bishop or pieces of local or national news that had come his way. Furthermore, the regular Sunday 'programme' was rather more elaborate than Catholics have become used to in more recent centuries. The parish clergy were required to recite in church Mattins (i.e. the Night Office plus Morning Prayer), Mass (sung) and Evensong (Vespers) in the afternoon. But since episcopal visitations too often recorded the complaints of the parishioners that the parish priest did not recite the offices they were evidently sometimes wanting. On the other hand, the great seasons and feasts of the year were marked by many a local custom – 'church ales' in the churchyard – that lightened the religion of medieval people and did something to connect worship with the life they lived day by day. As the Middle Ages came towards their end, however, other factors came into play that brought new and not always desirable emphases in worship.

Although the effects of the Black Death that ravaged Europe before and after 1348 must not be exaggerated, it seems to mark the beginning of the decline of European civilisation. Monasteries, friaries and convents were devastated by death and for some years the number and quality of the secular clergy diminished considerably. Nation-states like England and France were constantly at war and their internecine conflicts had their counterpart in the unceasing and ever more sterile disputes of the theological schools. As for the people, they were filled with fear generated by plague and war and almost desperately sought security. There is a dark streak in the Christianity of the late Middle Ages.

This situation affected popular piety and, to some extent, the liturgy. Emphasis on the physical sufferings of Christ became marked and in northern Europe Our Lady appears more and more as the Mother of Sorrows. People's fear of death, judgement and hell led to an increase of Masses for the dead and great numbers of priests said such Masses in the innumerable chantry chapels that filled the churches. Masses with only a single server present became ever more common. In monasteries and cathedrals the Mass was still celebrated with great pomp and ceremony but it did not touch the personal lives of the people, who increasingly sought the satisfaction of their spiritual needs outside the liturgy. Processions and pilgrimages multiplied, and the devotion of the Stations of the Cross (not yet fourteen) had made its way from Jerusalem to Europe by the fifteenth century. The Rosary appeared in the fifteenth century almost in the form we have known it (at first there were no 'mysteries'), and became very popular. But all these devotions tended to put the emphasis on externals, so that popular piety was a very busy affair.

A reaction came in the Netherlands with the *Devotio moderna,* which fostered meditation and recollection and, understandably, showed no great liking for the liturgical celebrations of the time. There were, as we have observed, private Masses in chapels where people on week-days could go and say their own prayers and, if they were literate, read the Prymers (collections of prayers, psalms and 'little offices') that began to appear at the time. Daily Mass for the laity began to be a feature of Catholic life. We remember that St Thomas More went to Mass frequently during the week, daily, according to one biographer.

Attendance at such Masses must have been a relief from the High Mass, which at times suggested confusion rather than liturgy. Over the centuries the practice of introducing phrases into the official texts had become prevalent. This was known as 'farcing' or 'stuffing' the texts. This can still be gathered from the book

53

called the *Kyriale,* where the *Kyrie* has a name attached to it, e.g. *Fons bonitatis* (Fount of goodness). But these and similar insertions were once *sung*, sometimes in the vernacular, and when to this was added figured music you sometimes had four things happening at once: the plainsong, the Latin words, the harmonies of the figured music and the vernacular texts. It must have been an awful noise, completely obscuring the message of the words.

Two further features illustrate the state of the liturgy in the later Middle Ages. Communion was for the most part still infrequent, though there was a trend in some places towards more frequent reception. But out of the institution of the Feast of Corpus Christi (1264), the formularies of which (some written by St Thomas Aquinas) give a profound and balanced teaching on the whole of the eucharist, there came, especially in northern Europe, first the procession of the Blessed Sacrament (fourteenth century) and then expositions of the sacrament during Mass. This is now forbidden, and Rome was always very sparing of permissions for this practice. At the same time began the practice of reserving the Blessed Sacrament in a prominent place. For centuries kept in the sacristy (as it still is on the last days of Holy Week), it came to be reserved in columns, in hanging pyxes, in niches in the church wall (Scotland), and finally, in tabernacles, which in the sixteenth century were put on the altar. Rome was the last place to adopt this practice. The emphasis, then, fell more and more on the Real Presence, which is but one aspect of the eucharist. Indeed, it could be said that by the end of the Middle Ages and *in practice* it had fallen into three parts: adoration of the Real Presence (the elevations, expositions, etc.); communion, often received apart from the Mass; the Mass as a sacrifice for the procuring of certain benefits. It was undue emphasis on this last that earned the condemnation of the Council of Trent.

The later Middle Ages were marked by a spirit of gain, the bourgeoisie was emerging and with them what historians call pre-capitalism. What the Mass could 'gain' for you became increasingly important, and strange practices grew up, later characterised by the Council of Trent as superstitious. Masses said consecutively over a number of days – seven, thirty (a 'mystical' number), forty or forty-four, for example – or said with a particular number of candles, were regarded as peculiarly efficacious. There were those who believed that if they attended Mass, or even simply saw the host, they would not grow older that day, that they would not fall ill, that in fact a whole range of material benefits would accrue to them. These Masses were often said in disorderly fashion in holes and corners by unbeneficed priests for a stipend. A whole proletariat of such priests swarmed throughout Europe at this time, and the Council of Trent did its best to suppress them. As Father Jungmann has said, the Mass came to be looked upon as a 'good work', or even as a machine for the production of more 'good works', and he quotes Luther, who said that under the papacy you could buy merit or merit heaven with human 'good works'.[1]

The pity of it all is that there was an abundance of faith, there was the spiritual renewal among the Brethren of the Common Life in the Netherlands (the milieu from which the *Imitation of Christ* came), and among the monasteries of Italy and elsewhere. But the liturgy, untidy, overlaid with irrelevant song, spurious texts and unauthorised prayers, clericalised, and by its rite and language remote from the people, no longer provided a mould into which this new life could flow. And if the above account seems too gloomy and condemnatory, let it be remembered that a commission of the Fathers of the Council of Trent drew up a list of seventy-eight 'abuses' which they said must be abolished.

[1] J. A. Jungmann, *Pastoral Liturgy* (Eng. trans. London, 1962), p. 72.

7.

The Council of Trent and Liturgical Reform

Given the disarray and indeed chaos of the late Middle Ages, liturgical reform had become a necessity. After repeated false starts, the Council of Trent met in 1545 for the first of its three sessions (1545–8, 1551–2, 1562–3). But liturgical reform was not high on the Council's agenda. It was not until 1562, the year before the Council closed, that the Fathers began to discuss the doctrine of the Mass and its liturgy. They soon realised, however, that a general council is not the proper body to carry out liturgical reform and they committed the work to the papacy. They did however deal with three matters of liturgical interest.

The work of the Council

(1) They considered the list of abuses drawn up by the commission of the Council Fathers, but felt they could not deal with each one individually. They therefore issued a decree in which they condemned all superstitious practices and the more flagrant abuses of liturgical law or decorum.

(2) They discussed the matter of the language of the liturgy, and decided that the use of the vernacular was 'not expedient' at that time, when the Reformers had made the hearing of God's word and a comprehensible liturgy a point of doctrine (if you could not hear the word, they said, you could not be saved). It was a mild enough decision, and it is interesting to learn that the only English prelate present at the council, Thomas Goldwell, Bishop (in exile) of St Asaph, pleaded in the debate that some of the Mass should be in the language

of the people, since the gospel, especially, but also 'many other things', could be of spiritual profit to the people. In this context the Council Fathers urged pastors to explain (and, inevitably, translate!) during the celebration of Mass its texts and rites.

(3) The Council laid a very heavy emphasis on the duty of bishops and priests to preach the word of God. It was 'a primary duty', but the hopes of the Fathers were not fulfilled in any adequate fashion until the setting up of well organised seminaries in the seventeenth century.

As for doctrine, the Council produced, among other things, a serene and balanced theology of the eucharistic sacrifice which, if read and known, would save many today from over-emphatic statements on the subject.

The Pius V Missal

The liturgical commission set up by the pope set to work at once, and finished its most important tasks, the revision of the missal and the breviary, in the reign of Pius V (d. 1572). Although we do not know a great deal about the work of the commission we can detect two guiding principles.

The first was uniformity which, it should be remarked, was now possible thanks to the invention of printing in the previous century. All rites that could not claim two hundred years existence were swept away (Milan, the Carthusians, the Dominicans and one or two others claimed exemption). Prefaces and Sequences, a luxuriant growth, were severely pruned, and all farcings, adventitious prayers and spurious texts were suppressed. The Mass was now set in a rigid structure of rubrics to ensure that every priest said the same words and did the same things in the same way everywhere.

The second principle was simply conservation. It was no fault of the revisers that the rite as they restored it was that of the twelfth century, with all its accretions from Gallican and German sources. The science of liturgy had not yet come into being, and though they consulted 'old codices' they had to hand only such Roman documents as were then known. In fact, the missal of 1570, with three or four unimportant changes, was a copy of the first printed missal of 1474. *The Introibo* with its accompanying prayers was now officially attached to the Mass, a blessing was added at the end, and (illogically) after the dismissal, the 'Last Gospel' (John 1.1–14), which previously had been recited by the priest on his way back to the sacristy. In spite of the protests, expressed in the list of abuses, that the prayers at the offertory which speak of bread as 'this spotless host' and of the wine as the 'chalice of salvation' were inappropriate because misleading, the revisers retained and made an official part of the rite the six prayers said at this time, as well as the three before communion and the 'Lord I am not worthy', which remained as a private devotion of the priest. Even the extensive corpus of rubrics was adapted from a set drawn up earlier in the century.

A word or two must be said about these rubrics as they indicate the mind of the revisers. They are entirely centred upon the priest and what he has to do throughout the rite, and they give the distinct impression that the primary rite of the Roman liturgy is the Low Mass. It now becomes a matter of law that he must say everything that anyone else says or sings, even the introit long after the choir have finished singing it. In this vast body of rubrics the people are only mentioned twice, first, when the priest is told to show the host and chalice to them at the elevation, and secondly, when it is said, '*If* there are any to go to communion . . .', then he gives it to them. But strange thing, in the 1570 missal there is no rite for the administration of communion to the people. This, with its confession, absolution, the 'Behold the Lamb of God . . .', with the 'Lord I am not worthy . . .' and 'The Body of our Lord . . .', were added only after the publication of the *Rituale Romanum* (1614), when these texts were taken from the Rite of the Communion of the Sick.

Such, in brief, was the book that was imposed for the first time in history on the whole of the Latin Church. A considerable improvement on what had preceded it, the rite it presents is sober and even austere. In spite of accretions, it remained distinctly Roman, especially in the Canon, the prefaces, and the variable prayers, some of which go back to the fifth century. One weakness was its lectionary, which it simply took over from the Middle Ages. The readings were often badly divided, some beginning in the middle of a sentence, and since they had been inaccurately collated in the Middle Ages the epistle frequently did not correspond with the gospel. Again, on paper the rite was good enough, but the revisers do not seem to have reflected on the absurdity of certain dislocations that were written into the rite and made a matter of law; for example, after the rite has been in progress for several minutes ('the prayers at the foot of the altar'), the celebrant must go up to the altar to recite the *entrance* chant. Likewise the *Sanctus*, when sung, overlaid the Canon, so that not only could the people not hear the latter, they could not follow it either. In fact, the Canon came to be drowned in the ever more elaborate music that developed in the next four centuries. These weaknesses and many more became acutely obvious when, under the impact of the instructions of Pius X (1903), people were urged to take an active part in the celebration of the Mass. The difficulties the rite created stemmed from the fact that it was a priest's rite and, in practice, if not in intent, the people were excluded from it.

To end this section on a more positive note the revision of the sixteenth century, imperfect as it was, can be seen to have been providential. The coming centuries were not at all propitious for the liturgy and, in spite of everything that people at different times tried to do to it, the rite remained intact.

Post-Tridentine vicissitudes

There can be little doubt that Pius V meant that the revised liturgy as represented by his breviary and missal (1568 and 1570 respectively) should have a long life. But succeeding popes did not feel bound by his work. Because medieval calendars had become over-loaded with saints' feasts, many of which were celebrated on a Sunday, the revisers had cut down their number to 182, most of which were *not* intended to be celebrated on a Sunday. In this way they largely restored the old Roman liturgical year. But Pius V's successors began to put them back again. Sixtus V (d. 1590), a Franciscan, restored to the calendar St Antony of Padua and St Francis of Paola (both Franciscans), as well as the Presentation of the Blessed Virgin Mary. And so it went on, until in our own time nearly every day in the year had its saint's feast, and sometimes several that had to be commemorated on the same day. Great numbers of men and women have of course been canonised since the sixteenth century, and if the Church was not to look like a museum it was right and proper that they should be commemorated in the liturgy. But many had little relevance to the life of the whole Church, and in the recent revision these have been allotted to local calendars or to those of the religious orders which would honour them.

In the period from 1570 to about 1960 there was also a multiplication of 'votive' Masses intended to allow the expression of certain popular devotions. These could, and often did, supersede the Mass of the day, so that in Lent, for example, instead of the Lenten Masses with their ancient course of readings and collects, numerous Masses with titles such as the Holy Winding Sheet, the Sacred Lance and the like blotted out the liturgy of the season. The liturgy had begun once again to look as untidy as it had done in the late Middle Ages.

This period has been described as 'the age of changelessness and rubricism'. It was not quite so changeless as that dictum would seem to indicate, and it soon began to appear that the strict code of rubrics that was appended to the missal was defective. Two popes, Clement VIII (d. 1605) and Urban VIII (d. 1644), had the rubrics revised and the latter (within sixty years of Pius V's revision!) spoke of the 'degeneration' that had set in and determined to remedy it. But certain basic weaknesses of the rubrics remained. A 'double' feast of a saint could oust the Sunday Mass, and since the office of a saint was shorter than that of the Sunday the clergy as a whole opted for the saint's feast. It was through a similar weakness of the rubrics that the votive Masses came to dominate seasons like Lent and Advent.

Change consisted of additions. It was only in 1752 that the preface of the Trinity was ordered to be said on the Sundays after Epiphany and Pentecost. The preface of St Joseph and that for Masses of the Dead were inserted into the meagre collection of the missal in 1919, and those for Christ the King and the Sacred Heart appeared as late as 1926 and 1928. The inclusion of over eighty prefaces in the missal of 1970 marks a return to sixth century practice, when almost every Mass had its own. There were also, of course, new Mass formularies for the numerous new feasts of various sorts that were instituted during the modern period. A different kind of addition that could hardly be said to be liturgical was the attachment to Low Mass by Leo XIII in 1884 of the 'Prayers after Mass'. From 1870 to 1929 the pope was 'the prisoner of the Vatican' and the intention of the prayers was 'the Liberty of the Church', later changed to 'Prayers for Russia'. Although they were never an official part of the rite many thought they were, and were aggrieved when they became obsolete after 1960.

Elsewhere there were developments of a different sort. In France in the late seventeenth century and in the first half of the eighteenth, the Church there, basing itself on its 'Gallican liberties', revised and, as it thought, improved the Roman books and produced what are known as the 'Neo-Gallican liturgies'. In the Germanies of the eighteenth century, the so-called Age of Enlightenment, which affected the Church as well as secular society, there was a strong feeling against mystery in general and the obscurity of the Mass in particular. Vernacular texts overlaid the Latin texts and the Germans claimed, with some reason, that they were continuing a medieval tradition. In the nineteenth century and in the first part of the twentieth the custom of singing vernacular hymns and vernacular paraphrases of the official texts during Mass was widespread in German-speaking countries. These customs, undesirable as they were, are indications that the rite was too rigid and that its language had become remote from the people.

It was not until Pius X (d. 1914), with his decrees on frequent communion and communion for young children and his letter on church music (1903), in which he urged that the people should take an active part in the Mass by singing it, that the first signs of change began to appear. He made beneficial changes in the Divine Office, and by a re-ranking of saints' feasts as well as of votive Masses he made it possible to celebrate the liturgical year as it should be. The war of 1914–1918 cut short his work, which, however, had made an entirely new edition of the missal necessary. This appeared in 1920.

Meanwhile the pastoral liturgical movement had got under way, thanks to the vision and energy of Dom Lambert Beauduin of the Abbey of Mont-César in Belgium. The emphasis at first was on active participation by singing the Latin texts, *Gloria, Sanctus,* etc., but Dialogue Masses (in which the people answered the priest when he spoke to them: 'The Lord be with *you*', and prayed with him in, e.g. the *Gloria*) began in the 1920s and received a somewhat cautious authorisation from Rome in 1935. The practice became widespread during and after the war in the armed forces, in schools, colleges, universities and Catholic Action circles.

After the war the liturgical movement became ever stronger in the Church, and the emphasis on the pastoral aspect of worship increased. Its aim at first was to help people to understand their liturgy and to encourage them to take part by word and song. But these very efforts revealed that the rite as it then was made both understanding and participation difficult. It was in this way that requests for reform came to be made. The first fruits were the restoration of the Easter Vigil in 1951, the complete revision of the Holy Week liturgy in 1955, which now became obligatory, and permission for Masses in the evening and a gradual relaxation of the eucharistic fast. As is well known, the Second Vatican Council, endorsing so much that had already been done, decreed the reform of the Roman liturgy, a reform that has been carried out between the years 1964 and 1974 and is not yet quite complete.

8.

The Order of the Mass of 1970

Although the rite now in use is well known it may be helpful to readers to have a brief *historical* commentary on it, which will serve to summarise a good deal of the foregoing history. The official commentary giving the *meaning* of the rite is to be found in the *General Instruction on the Roman Missal.*[1]

The Introductory Rites

These are more extensive than ever before and include everything from the entrance chant to the opening prayer (collect). Of these, the entrance chant (now often a hymn) and the collect represent fifth century practice. The sign of the cross and the confession come from late medieval usage and were made an official part of the Mass with the missal of 1570. The *Kyries* reflect the change made by Gregory the Great in the late sixth century when they were sung any number of times. The ninefold *Kyrie* was a later (Gallican) practice.

The 'Glory be to God on high', an ancient Greek text first used in morning prayer both in the East and the West, was introduced into the Mass in the fifth century but its use was restricted to the Feast of Christmas and might be intoned only by a bishop. Its use was gradually extended to Easter, Sundays and feasts of martyrs. It was only in the eleventh century that the priest was allowed to intone it, a custom that became general in the twelfth.

The formal greeting 'The Lord be with you', biblical in origin, is as old as the fourth century when, in Africa at least, it opened

[1] English translation, Clifford Howell, S.J., CTS Do 455, 1973.

the service, the readings following immediately.[2] The recommendation of the General Instruction (n. 86) that the celebrant or another should introduce the Mass of the day in his own words is new.

The liturgy of the word

The pattern of this part of the Mass adopted by the Order of 1970 is most probably the one in use in the late fourth century. If the responsorial psalm did not always follow the first Old Testament reading, the Alleluia was, in both East and West, always attached to the proclamation of the gospel. It is a solemn introduction to it, and that is why a sentence from the gospels (on the greater feasts from the gospel of the day) is sung with the Alleluias. The procession to the place of proclamation is found both in the East and the West ('Christ is still proclaming his gospel' (CL n. 33) and it is he who is being honoured). The candles that are carried are a sign of joy (though this does not seem to be a primitive Roman custom; they are not carried at the Easter Vigil). In the seventh century a thurifer with smoking thurible formed part of the procession but the book was not incensed. The acclamations before and after the gospel, 'Glory to you, Lord', and, 'Praise to you, Lord Jesus Christ', were adopted by Rome from the Gallican rite.

The *homily,* an integral part of the rite, is also one of its oldest elements, as we have shown above.

(The Dismissal of the Catechumens. As long as there was a catechumenate the catechumens were dismissed after the ministry of the word. In some places the practice lasted until the twelfth century, although there were no longer any catechumens. It is of interest to us today, for the word used in the West was *'missa (est)'* or *dimissio'.* From the former word comes 'Mass'.)

The *Creed* was inserted into the Roman Mass in 1014. The plural form, 'We believe . . .', is that of the second ecumenical Council of Constantinople of 381. The whole assembly is declaring its assent to the one faith.

---

[2] The first alternative greeting, 'The grace of our Lord Jesus Christ . . .', comes from II Corinthians 13.13, and the second, 'The grace and peace . . .', from Ephesians 1.2. The reply is from I Peter 1.3: 'Blessed be God, the Father of our Lord Jesus Christ.'

As we have seen, the *Prayer of the Faithful* goes back to the earliest centuries of the Church. The form has varied and the one now in use (except for Good Friday) is related to late fifth century models which were translated from the Greek.

The liturgy of the eucharist

This consists of the Preparation of the Gifts, the eucharistic prayer and holy communion.

The *Preparation of the Gifts,* still often called the offertory, has been remodelled. Its essential elements are the bringing of the bread and wine to the altar, the singing of a processional chant and the final (variable) prayer, called the 'prayer over the offerings'. The other prayers are intended for the priest's private devotion. The two over the bread and wine respectively *may* be said aloud when there is no singing. They are modelled on Jewish table-prayers (cf. Chapter 1). The other two, 'By the mystery of this water and wine', and, 'Lord God, we ask you to receive us', come from the medieval collections.

Incensation of the gifts and the altar

In the Roman tradition incense was burned in great braziers and was carried only at the entrance procession, at the singing of the gospel and at the end of the service. Incensation of objects, of the altar and the gifts lying on it, only came into use in the Frankish empire in the early ninth century. It was adopted later in Rome. Its intention is to enhance the offering that is being made and serves to remind worshippers of the heavenly liturgy of which the earthly is a reflection (cf. Apocalypse 5.8: '... each one of them ... had a golden bowl full of incense made of the prayers of the saints'). The most important of the incensations and the oldest is that of the altar and its gifts at the offertory. The custom of incensing people (celebrant, ministers and people) is found in the eleventh century, though that does not mean that it was common to all celebrations everywhere.

The washing of the hands

The history of this simple gesture is a little complicated. It used to be said that the priest needed to wash his hands after handling

65

the offerings (and/or thurible). But this will not do, for in the former pontifical Mass the bishop washed his hands at the *beginning* of the offertory act and again at its end. The former washing derives from the seventh century Roman rite, when the bishop received the offerings, washed his hands and then sang the prayer over the offerings. The second washing appears in the Roman rite only in the fourteenth century, and it is this one that has survived. For Jungmann its meaning is that now the celebrant is entering the zone of holiness and he wishes to purify himself before doing so,[3] as the formula accompanying this gesture shows (a verse from psalm 50; formerly from psalm 25: 'I will wash my hands among the innocent'). It is a Gallican notion unknown to the earlier Roman rite.

The 'Orate Fratres'

The invitatory that follows 'Pray, brethren . . .' (in the Sarum rite 'Pray brothers and sisters') also has a complicated history. Known as long ago as the eighth century, it was uttered after the offerings had been collected, when the celebrant turned to his fellow-clergy standing round and asked for prayers 'to offer to the Lord the oblation of the people'. The presentation of the offerings was still practised. But for several centuries there was no reply (as in the Carthusian and Dominican rites). Later, when Low Masses became common, the invitatory was addressed to the people and a reply was expected, though this was three verses of psalm 19. It was not until the eleventh century that a reply similar to the one still used came into use in certain parts of Italy and was then adopted by Rome. Even so, the response was in fact made by a clerical choir.

The prayer over the offerings

This (variable) prayer was the only offertory prayer known to the early Roman rite. It is almost certain that it was in the Frankish realm that it began to be called (*oratio*) *secreta,* a prayer to be said in a low voice. It is now clear that it should be understood as the 'prayer over the offerings' (*oratio super oblata,* as in the current Roman Missal). Originally sung or recited aloud it became silent, perhaps under the influence of the practice of reciting the

[3] J. A. Jungmann, *The Mass of the Roman Rite,* pp. 349–352.

Canon in a low voice or even silently. In some books the whole Canon was called *Secreta*. The prayer summed up the whole offertory act, as it still does.

The eucharistic prayers

Sufficient has been said about the Roman Canon above. All we need to comment on here is the expression '*mysterium fidei*' which is found inserted in the words of the consecration of the wine in the seventh century edition of the Canon. It is thought, with some probability, to be the pious exclamation of a copyist who put it in the margin, from which it got into the text. Or it may have been uttered by the deacon. It has been incorporated into the invitation to the acclamation: 'Let us proclaim the *mystery of faith*'.

Eucharistic Prayer II is, as we have seen, based on the prayer of Hippolytus.

Eucharistic Prayer III is a modern composition (by Dom Cipriano Vagaggini), which incorporates a text from the Mozarabic liturgy: 'Father, you are holy indeed . . . to the glory of your name', and one or two phrases from the eastern and Gallican liturgies: e.g. 'On the *night* he was betrayed'.

Eucharistic Prayer IV is modelled on the Antiochene prayers (e.g. St John Chrysostom's) though with the insertion of a pre-consecration *epiclesis* from the Egyptian tradition. It has no variable preface and in the first part there is a thanksgiving for creation, and it develops the history of salvation at some length. It has some short passages from a fourth century prayer of St Basil and numerous scriptural references both explicit and implicit.

As well as the pre-consecration *epiclesis* of the Holy Spirit all these prayers have another after the consecration which is an invocation for a fruitful communion. This, and the grouping of the intercessions at the end of the prayers, corresponds with the Antiochene pattern. All have deep roots in the past.

The rite of communion

This has been much simplified. The Lord's Prayer now clearly appears as the first prayer before communion, the *embolism* has been shortened and the breaking of the bread transferred to where it belongs, after the sign of peace, so that the *Agnus Dei* ('Lamb of God . . .') once again accompanies the breaking of the bread. A response has been inserted at the end of the *embolism* ('. . . the coming of our Saviour, Jesus Christ'): 'For the kingdom, the power and the glory . . .'. This phrase, found in certain Greek MSS of St Matthew's gospel, may well be a Jewish doxology with which certain prayers ended. It has parallels in the early Christian document called the *Didache (The Teaching of the Twelve Apostles)*. The sign of peace, re-attached to 'The peace of the Lord be with you always', has now been restored to the people. Perhaps most important of all, the communion of priest and people now forms one rite.

The mingling of the host and the consecrated wine

This has been described as the most difficult ceremony of the Mass to explain. It is a very ancient rite. As early as the second century it was customary for the pope to send to other bishops a portion of the consecrated host as a sign of unity. Later, whenever the pope celebrated he sent similar portions to the priests of the titular churches which they put into the chalice. In the seventh century there were two minglings, the first after the words, 'The peace of the Lord be with you all', when it was a part of a pre-consecrated host that was dropped in the chalice, and the second when immediately before communion the pope detached a piece from his own host and put it in the chalice. These two actions were fused into one in the Carolingian period because the second was a purely Roman custom and was not fully understood. Later still, in the tenth century, its meaning was forgotten altogether and its interpretation was not made easier by the formula that had been attached to it: 'May this mingling and *consecration* of the Body and Blood of our Lord Jesus Christ bring eternal life to those who receive (them)'. The Council of Trent objected to the word 'consecration' but it was retained, and in fact means 'sanctification' or 'hallowing'. It has been removed from the present rite and the formula now reads, 'May this mingling of the body and blood of our Lord Jesus Christ bring eternal life to us who receive it'.[4] This takes us back to the origins of the rite and before

---

[4] The translation ought to read 'them' for the phrase refers back to the body and blood.

a symbolic meaning was imposed on it: in the ancient Syrian rite from which it comes its purpose was to facilitate the giving of communion in both kinds. The people received both the Body and Blood together in one action.

The administration of holy communion

The procession, the song and reception of the bread in the hand are at least as old as the fourth century. There is a particularly vivid description of the rite in the *Lectures on the Sacraments* attributed to St Cyril of Jerusalem, also of the fourth century. The communicants are instructed to make the right hand a throne with hollowed palm, to say 'Amen' when receiving, to hallow the eyes by touching them with the bread and then to eat it. When they receive from the cup they say 'Amen', receive, and, while the moisture is on their lips, they are to touch it and then their eyes and forehead. Whatever is to be thought of this practice it is a witness to the profound devotion with which Christians of that time received holy communion.

The formulas 'The body of Christ' and 'The blood of Christ' are also of the fourth century (St Ambrose gives the first verbatim), and may be of the third.

It is worth noting that all the words that immediately precede the reception of communion are taken from holy scripture: 'Behold the Lamb of God . . .', John 1:28; 'Lord, I am not worthy . . .', Matthew 8:8; 'Happy are those who are called to his supper', Apocalypse 19:9. This last is an addition and indicates that the eucharist is the anticipation of the heavenly banquet.

The dismissal

There were many formulas of blessing in the medieval books but the blessing was given *before* communion. New ones have been provided in the 1970 rite. The dismissal, as is but logical, comes last.

Glossary

Although almost all technical terms and Latin phrases have been explained in the text a glossary gathering them together may be useful for reference.

Alleluia A Hebrew word meaning 'Praise the Lord'. Certain psalms sung after the Passover meal were called 'Hallel' psalms. See Matthew 26:10.

Ambo A sort of pulpit for the reading of the scriptures.

Amen Another Hebrew word which means giving one's assent to anything said or done by another: e.g. the great Amen at the end of the eucharistic prayer. It is stronger in meaning than 'So be it'.

Anamnesis A Greek word used of the section of the eucharistic prayer following the institution narrative: 'We recall or make the memorial of . . .', that is, we bring before God the saving work of his Son Jesus in his passion, death and resurrection and because we do this at the command of Jesus the power of his redeeming work is made present to us.

Canon A Greek word meaning 'rule'; in the Roman liturgy the eucharistic prayer that is 'the rule'. At first it was used with the word 'action': 'Here begins the Canon of the (eucharistic) action' that is to follow. It was 'the rule' in another sense: the eastern eucharistic prayers did not and do not admit of any variability. When a change is desired the whole prayer is changed: e.g. in the Ethiopian rite there are some eighteen prayers. 'Canon' then in the West came to be regarded as the 'fixed rule' varied only by the 'prefaces' and *embolisms* (q.v.) within the Canon. It applies properly only to the Roman eucharistic prayer. The other three in the missal are called 'eucharistic prayers'; e.g. *Prex Euchar-istica* II.

70

Collect From *collecta*, a late Latin word derived from *collectio* (*colligere* = to collect). It is the opening prayer of the Mass in which the president 'collects' or gathers up the intentions of the people. In Rome itself the word *collecta* could mean the *place* of assembly.

Catechumens A Greek word meaning 'those under instruction'. The catechumenate usually lasted three years, the last part taking place in Lent. Catechumens were dismissed after the homily. Hence this part of the Mass came to be called 'The Mass of the Catechumens'. They were received into the Church at the Easter Vigil (or sometimes at Whitsun) by baptism, confirmation and holy communion.

Communicantes ('In union with the whole Church'). The third section of the Roman Canon after the *Sanctus*.

Doxology From the Greek *doxa* 'glory': giving glory to God, as in the last sentence of the eucharistic prayer but also in the *Gloria in excelsis* (the greater doxology) and in the 'Glory be to the Father . . .' (the lesser doxology). It is a translation of the Hebrew word *Kabod,* very important in the Old Testament. Cf. the *Sanctus*, Isaiah 6:3.

Ember Days 'Ember' is from an Old English ('Anglo-Saxon') word meaning fasting. They occurred on the Wednesdays, Fridays and Saturdays (when a vigil was kept) in the spring, in September and December. The Lent Ember Days were a later addition. Ember Days were among the oldest of the Roman observances, dating back to the fourth century, and were concerned with the various seasonal harvests. In the new liturgy they have been replaced with a twice-annual observance when prayers are offered for human work and the needy.

Embolism A Greek word meaning something 'thrown in', i.e. an insertion. Examples are the insertions in the *Communicantes* on certain feast days and the prayer after the Lord's Prayer.

Epiclesis A Greek word meaning 'invocation', used of the calling down of the Holy Spirit on the bread and wine and the communicants in the course of the eucharistic prayer. There are invocations in the Roman Canon before and after the institution narrative though they do not mention the Holy Spirit.

Epiphany (The *Manifestation* of the Lord). In the 1570 missal (and previously) the Sundays in the early part of the year until Septuagesima (third Sunday before Lent) were called the 'Sundays after Epiphany'. When Easter was late there were six of them.

The Eucharistic Prayer This is the usual term for the prayer that begins with the dialogue, 'The Lord be with you ... Lift up your hearts', and ends with the doxology, 'Through him, with him, in him ...'. It is applicable to both eastern and western liturgies, though in the East it is called *anaphora,* from *ana-pherein,* to offer up.

Gaul Gallia was the old Roman name for what is now France, though under that term it included more, and the frontiers in the south between France and Spain varied in the Middle Ages. It was in Southern Gaul that a liturgy developed usually known as 'Gallican'. It was ancient and had certain eastern features, some adopted from Spain (which continued to have contacts with the Middle East). With the conquests of Charlemagne in the eighth century Gaul became part of the Frankish empire which extended east into the Germanies, not yet a single nation. Gallican, Spanish and German elements contributed to the formation of the liturgy as we have come to know it.

Hanc igitur ('Father accept this offering'). The fourth section of the Roman Canon after the *Sanctus.*

Hosanna A Hebrew word meaning 'Save, we pray' but which came to be used simply as an acclamation. Cf. Matthew 21:9.

Institution Narrative This term, almost always used by liturgists nowadays, is the equivalent of 'the words of consecration'. These however differ in the various New Testament accounts of the institution of the eucharist and from one liturgy to another.

Liturgy A Christianised Greek word meaning the public worship of the Church described in the Constitution on the Liturgy (n. 7) as 'The whole public worship performed by the mystical body of Jesus Christ, that is, by the head and his members.' The term covers the content of the liturgy and its celebration (see 'rite'). In the Byzantine and some other eastern rites the celebration of the eucharist is called 'The Liturgy' or 'The Divine Liturgy' as it is the Church's worship *par excellence.*

Mass From *mittere* (noun *missio*) = 'to send'. The term *missa est* was used to dismiss the catechumens after the homily. It came to be used for the dismissal at the end of the eucharist. St Ambrose is apparently the first to use it in this way. It has nothing to do with sending worshippers out on a mission. For centuries the term 'Mass' has been used of the whole of the eucharist and it has entered into all the Indo-European languages in various forms.

Ordo or **Order** Originally an 'order of service'. Later some of the texts of the liturgical service were included. In the new liturgy the Orders for the Mass, the other sacraments and liturgical rites include a general instruction, directives about the celebration of the rite and the texts.

Pentecost In the former missal the Sundays after Pentecost (Whitsunday) were called the 'Sundays after Pentecost' numbered according to the date of Easter from 24 to 28. In the Middle Ages after the feast of the Holy Trinity had been inserted into the calendar the Sundays were counted 'after Trinity' as in the Book of Common Prayer.

The Prayer of the Faithful (in England often called 'Bidding Prayers'; in the *Missale Romanum* called also *Oratio Universalis* for which the term 'The General Intercession' is used). The prayer consists of 'intentions' for which the people are invited to pray. The prayer is the response: e.g. 'Lord hear our prayer'. This may be varied.

Preface The first part of the eucharistic prayer and integral to it. It *may* mean 'proclamation' though this is not certain. In the Roman rite it does in fact proclaim and thank God for his saving deeds 'through Jesus Christ our Lord'.

Rite The manner or way of celebrating a liturgy. This was controlled by a very detailed set of rubrics (directives printed in *red*) in the 1570 missal. More flexible directives are given in the General Instruction to the Roman Missal of 1970. More broadly the word means a different ordering of the eucharist and other services: e.g. the Byzantine rite, the Coptic rite.

Sabaoth Hebrew word now translated in the *Sanctus* as 'hosts', i.e. heavenly armies or powers.

Te igitur (literally, 'Thee, therefore'); the first words of the Roman Canon after the *Sanctus*.

Use Conventionally this word is used of smaller variations within one rite: e.g. the rite of Sarum or Salisbury which was the Roman rite with some variations that did not affect its basic pattern.

Books for further reading

J. A. Jungmann, S.J., *The Mass of the Roman Rite*. Eng. trans. F. A. Brunner, revised by Charles K. Riepe (London, Burns and Oates, 1961). This is the single volume edition, without the lengthy footnotes and containing new material.

A. G. Martimort (ed.), *The Eucharist*. Eng. trans. of part of *L'Eglise en Prière* (1965) (Irish University Press, Shannon, Ireland, 1973). The clearest and most concise account of the Mass in the past and present.

J. D. Crichton, *Christian Celebration: The Mass* (London, Geoffrey Chapman, 1971). An extended commentary on the Mass, the Calendar and Missal of 1970.

Johannes H. Emminghaus, *The Eucharist*. Essence. Form, Celebration. Eng. trans. (The Liturgical Press, Collegeville, Minnesota, U.S.A., 1978).

General Instruction on the Roman Missal. Eng. trans. Clifford Howell, S.J. (CTS, 1973). This gives the *meaning* of the various elements of the Order of Mass of 1970 and the directives for celebrating it.

A most useful collection in translation of the principal eucharistic prayers both eastern and western: *Prayers of the Eucharist. Early and Reformed* (abbreviated PEER); eds. R. C. D. Jasper and G. J. Cuming (London, Collins, 1975).

Vatican II, *Constitution on the Sacred Liturgy (Sacrosanctum Concilium)*, CTS Do 386.